I0605544

CAN WE TALK?

How Humans Stay in Touch

Maria Birmingham

Illustrated by
Xulin

ORCA BOOK PUBLISHERS

Published in Canada and the United States in 2025 by Orca Book Publishers.
orcabook.com

Library and Archives Canada Cataloguing in Publication
Title: Can we talk? : how humans stay in touch / Maria Birmingham ; illustrated by Xulin.
Names: Birmingham, Maria, author. | Xulin, illustrator.
Series: Orca timeline ; 8.
Description: Series statement: Orca timeline ; 8 | Includes bibliographical references and index.
Identifiers: Canadiana (print) 20240319893 | Canadiana (ebook) 20240319907 |
ISBN 9781459838727 (hardcover) | ISBN 9781459838734 (PDF) | ISBN 9781459838741 (EPUB)
Subjects: LCSH: Communication—Juvenile literature. |
LCSH: Communication—History—Juvenile literature. | LCGFT: Informational works.
Classification: LCC P91.2 .B57 2025 | DDC j302.2—dc23

Library of Congress Control Number: 2024933245

Summary: Part of the nonfiction Orca Timeline series for middle-grade readers, this illustrated book examines how humans have communicated over time.

Orca Book Publishers is committed to reducing the consumption of nonrenewable resources in the production of our books. We make every effort to use materials that support a sustainable future.

Orca Book Publishers gratefully acknowledges the support for its publishing programs provided by the following agencies: the Government of Canada, the Canada Council for the Arts and the Province of British Columbia through the BC Arts Council and the Book Publishing Tax Credit.

Cover and interior artwork by Xulin.
Design by Dahlia Yuen.
Edited by Kirstie Hudson.

Printed and bound in South Korea.

28 27 26 25 • 1 2 3 4

For my writing buddy Charlotte,
who I miss more than words can say

Hands up! We sometimes use our communication skills to share information with others.
SKYNESHER/GETTY IMAGES

CONTENTS

INTRODUCTION 1

ONE 5
Now Hear This

TWO 17
Speak Up

THREE 29
Spread the Word

FOUR 41
Going the Distance

FIVE 55
Tech Talk

SIX 69
Computers Rule

GLOSSARY 81
RESOURCES 83
ACKNOWLEDGMENTS 84
INDEX 85

INTRODUCTION

Now You're Talking!

Humans are experts at ***communication***. We know how to stay in touch with each other—whether through our words or our actions. Think about your day so far and consider how many times you've communicated with someone. It might be a parent, a bus driver, a friend or even a pet. You may have used spoken words. You might have shrugged when asked a question. Or perhaps you fired off a quick text to say "hey." All of these instances are just a few of the ways you express yourself.

We have to communicate with others so we can let them know things like what we need or how we're feeling or simply to share ideas and connect. Today we have a variety of ways to stay in touch besides face-to-face conversations—like smartphones, texting apps and email. We can chat with Aunt Millie on the other side of the world. And we can do it instantaneously. Of course, early humans didn't have it so easy. If someone wasn't nearby—either close enough to see or hear—there was no chance for communication. Over time humans moved to new places, and different ***civilizations*** evolved. That made it even more difficult to stay connected. So we worked to figure out methods of long-distance communication to resolve the problem.

Connecting 24-7

With technology still something in the distant future, our ***ancestors*** used messages—both spoken and written—to keep in touch with those who were far away. They often relied on others to deliver these messages. But humans are a curious and creative bunch. So as the centuries moved along, we looked for faster ways to communicate over the miles. We learned to use things like electricity, invisible radio waves and even space satellites to send messages and information to far-off destinations. With helpful inventions like the telephone, which allowed us to chat with friends and family who lived elsewhere, along with radios and televisions, communication only got better. Then came a real game changer: computers. These machines gave us the capability to hop on the ***internet*** or send emails. Add to that the smartphone, which itself is really just a small computer. Besides making phone calls, it lets us chat through text messages, run apps and surf the Net. All of which means that today humans can connect with each other in an instant, 24 hours a day, every day of the week, if we choose. Communicating from a distance is now literally in the palm of our hands!

We spend a lot of our time communicating with our friends and those closest to us.
MOMO PRODUCTIONS/GETTY IMAGES

We're Not Finished Yet

We mostly take this ease of communication for granted. But if we really think about it, it's pretty remarkable how effortlessly we can connect with each other. Consider this: experts say that our earliest ancestors didn't even have the ability to speak. Yet somehow here we are today—a planet of people who can talk up a storm and use technology to connect us.

So where will communication go from here? Are we finished finding new ways to stay in touch? Not a chance. Who knows what's to come, but even today experts and scientists are working away on innovative ideas to help us stay connected. For instance, what would you think about meeting up with your best friend in the form of holograms? Holograms are 3D images that are visible without 3D glasses. You may be familiar with them from movies or TV shows. Some researchers are working to design a technology that would allow "hologram you" to have a get-together with the hologram version of a friend for a face-to-face conversation of sorts. Imagine that! But before we get too ahead of ourselves, let's take a step back and find out how we went from a population of nonspeakers to a bunch of folks who sometimes don't know when to quiet down. It's time to get to the bottom of it with some straight talk about the inventive—and sometimes unimaginable—ways that humans have kept in touch.

?
68,000 BCE
Early humans
begin to speak
2020
Scientists recreate
the voice of
Egyptian mummy
c.1980s
Scientists study
whether babies
recognize Mom's voice

ONE

NOW HEAR THIS

Our earliest human ancestors, who hadn't yet begun to speak, had to come up with a way to communicate with each other. We often imagine they first used sounds and grunts to get their messages across. We may even see this in the cartoons or movies we watch. But a 2022 study by a team of scientists at the University of Western Australia suggests this wasn't the case. Instead, the experts believe, ***prehistoric*** humans used hand ***gestures***—moving a part of the body like the fingers or hands to express an idea—as their earliest method of communication. And in studies with a group of volunteers, the scientists found that gesturing is a more successful way of conveying ideas to someone else than groaning or grunting. Their studies also found that using the hands to explain visually how to do something is more memorable than using sounds. So they've concluded that spoken ***language*** followed sometime later. While it's impossible to confirm their findings, it's an interesting theory.

FUTURE
Tech for communicating brain to brain with no talking

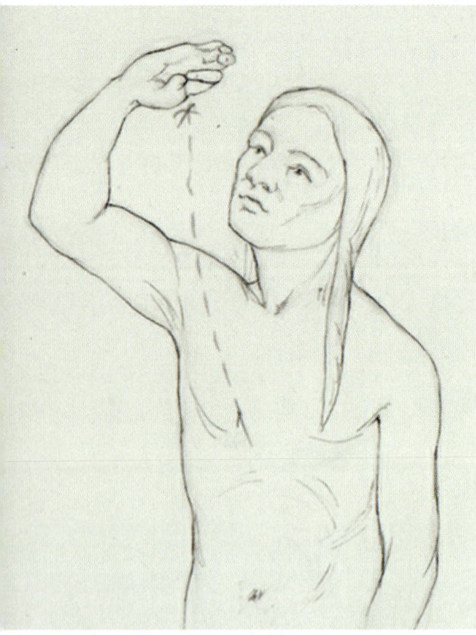

There are hundreds of sign languages used around the world. This example shows the sign for "noon" in Plains Sign Language.
GARRICK MALLERY/WIKIMEDIA COMMONS/PUBLIC DOMAIN

If These Hands Could Talk

We can see in today's world that gestures are still a valuable form of communication. Pay attention to what you do when you're telling someone a story. Chances are, you'll use hand gestures, as well as facial expressions and even the tone of your voice, to help make your story clearer.

Think about the gestures we commonly use to communicate. The thumbs-up signal, for example, says "well done" or "that's great." And then there's the peace sign, where you raise your palm outward and form a *V* with your index and middle finger. They're each a form of nonverbal communication. However, we need to be careful when using these signs. Like a spoken language, gestures can have different meanings in different parts of the world. For instance, the thumbs-up signal is acceptable in North America, but it's a rude gesture in parts of the Middle East.

Hand gestures are frequently used by people who are deaf or have hearing loss. There are more than 400 million people around the world who have some form of hearing loss. About 70 million are deaf. Many deaf people rely on sign language, using gestures rather than spoken words, to communicate. There are over 300 different sign languages in the world. Visual forms of language help ensure that there are no barriers in the community, providing equal opportunities to learn, work and live.

Thumbs-up! Sometimes we "speak" without words and let our hands do the talking.
TWINSTERPHOTO/GETTY IMAGES

Experts think prehistoric hand paintings like these from a cave in South America may have been used as a form of sign language.
R.M. NUNES/GETTY IMAGES

Ready to Chat

It's hard to pinpoint exactly when ancient humans moved past using gestures as their main form of communication and started to use speech as well. Experts don't agree on when it happened. Some suggest the first speech sounds were made hundreds of thousands of years ago. But others, such as George Poulos, a professor emeritus who works at the University of South Africa, believe it was more recent. He says humans began to speak about 70,000 years ago. How did he come up with this time frame? By analyzing human fossils, the ***anatomy*** of the body and human ***genes***, among other things. Poulos determined that the brain and vocal tract—which includes the mouth, throat, tongue and teeth—of early humans had developed enough by this point to create speech sounds.

WHAT'S THE WORD?

According to Poulos, these humans weren't instant chatterboxes who could immediately carry on a full-fledged conversation. He suggests the very first speech sound was more like a click. Think of it like a suction sound that you make with your tongue and the roof of your mouth. He says it was another 20,000 years before humans could produce other speech sounds, including a variety of consonants and vowels. These sounds were eventually used to form words. Poulos argues it was still another 30,000 years before a proper language with sentences evolved.

That said, it's worth noting that while Poulos's theory is intriguing, we have no way of knowing for sure whether his idea—or that of any other expert—is correct. Speech doesn't leave behind any evidence for scientists to unearth, so how language began is hard to determine. For this reason, experts can only make educated guesses and draw conclusions from their research. We will likely never know with absolute certainty when humans began to speak.

Why Talk?

While we can't say for sure when humans began to communicate with speech, it's interesting to think about *why* we began to use it. Why did we need to go beyond communicating through gestures? There are several theories about this. Some experts think that as humans began to use tools about 2.6 million years ago, their hands were busy, and this made communicating through gestures too difficult, so they gradually began to speak. Another theory is that humans needed to stay in touch when they couldn't see each other. They might have been too far apart to see someone's gesturing or perhaps the darkness of night made it impossible to communicate using their hands. And in order to survive in the harsh world, people needed to share information about things like food, water and shelter. Given that, experts theorize, humans had to find another way to "talk," and using their voices became a way to do just that.

Sharing information with each other is important when we need to work together to complete a task.
SOLSTOCK/GETTY IMAGES

Every human being has a unique voice. Experts say you usually recognize the voice of your closest friends and family quite easily.
FG TRADE/GETTY IMAGES

When boys begin ***adolescence*** around the age of 10, one of the changes they often experience is that their voices "crack" and "squeak" and eventually sound much deeper. That's because their vocal cords become longer and thicker at this age, which deepens the sound of their voice. Girls' voices also deepen around the same age, but the change is so minimal that you usually don't notice it.

The Sound of You

If we all produce a voice in the same way, why do we each have a unique voice? That comes down to the structure of our bodies. The throat, nostrils, tongue and mouth come in different shapes and sizes. And your vocal cords might be longer, thicker or tighter than those of other people. All these differences create voices that have different tones and a higher or lower sound. This makes for a voice that's all your own—and it's as unique as your fingerprints. In fact, some governments and companies now use special computer programs called voice-recognition systems that can identify a person simply by analyzing their voice.

TALK • ABOUT • IT

So how exactly do you speak? Here's what happens in your body when you produce your voice.

When you speak, air rushes from your lungs and goes up your windpipe to your voice box, or ***larynx***. It's that bony lump in the front your throat.

Inside the voice box are your vocal cords—small bands of muscle and tissue. The air from your lungs passes over the cords, making them vibrate and create sound waves.

These sound waves travel up through your throat into your mouth and nose. They leave your mouth as the sound of your voice.

You can change the flow of the air by using your tongue, lips and teeth. This produces different sounds.

Test your voice by making a variety of sounds, like *ahhhh*, *ooooh*, *teeee* and *laaaa*. Notice how you change the shape of your mouth and use your tongue and teeth differently to make each sound.

VOICE FROM THE PAST

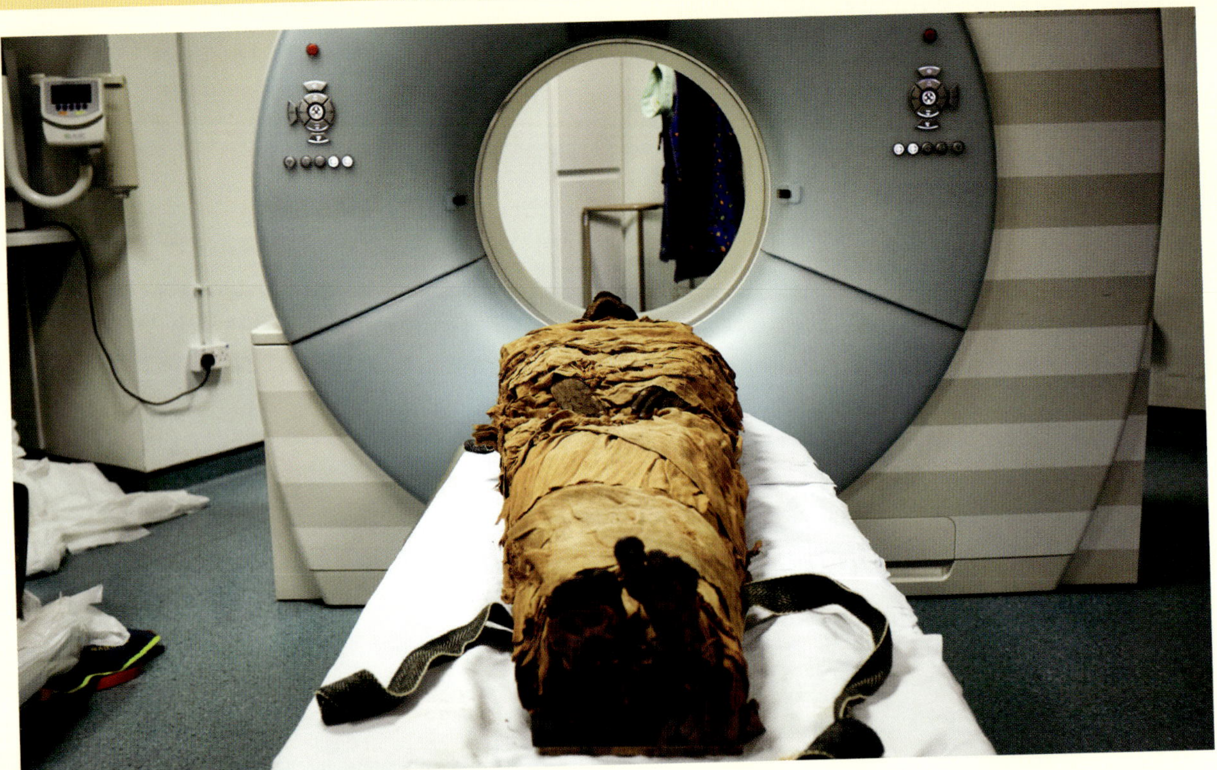

Meet the mummy! Researchers in London, England, used a special tunnel-like scanner to examine the larynx and throat of an ancient mummy. LEEDS MUSEUMS & GALLERIES

It speaks! In 2020 a team of ***archaeologists*** working at a university in England recreated the voice of an Egyptian mummy. The 3,000-year-old mummified person was an ancient priest named Nesyamun. The mummy was brought to a British museum about 200 years ago and has been the subject of many studies. In this instance, the scientists wanted to find a way to bring his voice back to life. It turned out his voice box and throat were intact thanks to an almost perfect mummification process. His tongue muscles were not so lucky and had dried up over time. But that didn't bother the scientists. They began by using medical scanners to get measurements of his vocal region. Then they recreated his voice box using a 3D printer. With that they were able to hook up the voice box to a loudspeaker and send an electronic signal through it to recreate Nesyamun's voice.

So what did this ancient mummy have to say? Not much, actually. In fact, you can't really describe the re-creation as a sentence or even a word. It was similar to a vowel-like groan. Imagine something like *eeuuughhh*. Funnily enough, you might say it resembled the moaning sound mummies in movies often make. The team said it was enough to give people a sense of how Nesyamun may have sounded and bring his voice to this century. The added benefit is that the technology could be used for future voice research.

Your voice box, or larynx, is a hollow tube in the middle of your throat that helps you make sounds. You can see or feel it on your neck.
DHARMAPADA BEHERA/GETTY IMAGES

Mom's the Word

Most of us recognize the voice of someone we know well, like a friend or family member. And it seems this holds true from the minute we're born—when it comes to our moms, anyway. Doctors have found that even one-day-old babies recognize their mom's voice. In a study by researchers Anthony DeCasper and William Fifer, newborns were given pacifiers connected to an ***audio***-playback device. The device played either their mom's voice or that of an unfamiliar woman, depending on whether the babies sucked on their pacifiers. The babies kept sucking when they were listening to their mom's voices. They learned after about 10 minutes that they could stop the playback of the unfamiliar voice by not sucking on their pacifiers for two seconds or more. So they adjusted their sucking behavior to hear their mom's voices.

According to the researchers, this study shows that newborns recognize their mother and prefer her voice over anyone else's. Interestingly, there's no sign that they recognize their father's or siblings' voices at this stage, even if they've heard them often while in their mom's belly. Experts say it probably helps that babies hear the sound of good ol' mom in two separate ways, through the belly while she speaks aloud, and through the vibrations of her vocal cords, which are felt elsewhere in her body.

BLUEFLAMES/ GETTY IMAGES

Have you ever seen someone inhale helium from a balloon and then start speaking with a squeaky voice? Here's the reason for that voice change. Helium is lighter than air. So sound waves travel twice as fast through it. When someone breathes in helium, the air from their lungs travels much more quickly across their vocal cords and gives it that squeaky sound. And while a few breaths of helium isn't usually a big deal, more than that can be dangerous, so it's probably best to leave helium in the balloon and out of you.

TELL ME MORE

Before they learn to speak, babies use gestures to communicate. At around nine months old, they may use common gestures like waving, pointing or clapping. And we still use gestures once we reach adulthood. Think about how we shrug or high-five someone as a form of communication.

Humans are expert communicators. We use a number of gestures to get our points across. You may notice this if you pay attention during a conversation.
(TOP) SRDJANPAV/GETTY IMAGES; (LEFT) HRAUN/GETTY IMAGES; (RIGHT) JOHN GIUSTINA/GETTY IMAGES

Don't Speak

Right now using our voices is our best way to communicate with people who are nearby. But researchers are studying new ways to help us connect, including allowing us to have conversations with friends without ever uttering a word. These experts are working to develop a technology that would enable our brains to send messages back and forth. Here's how it would work. You'd think a thought, and it would be sent to an electronic device. That device would record your brain's message, decode it and transmit it directly to your friend's brain. And vice versa. It'd be the quietest conversation ever! Of course, sending and receiving messages between brains might sound completely unimaginable to you, but get this. Over a decade ago, a team of researchers at the University of Washington successfully sent brain signals from one individual over the internet to control the hand movements of another person. Now one of these researchers is working on a method of transmitting information directly from one person's brain to the brain of another. So maybe having a conversation between brains is not quite as far-fetched as it sounds.

Could there come a time in the future when special technology inside our bodies will help us communicate?

COLIN ANDERSON PRODUCTIONS PTY LTD/GETTY IMAGES

c. 1500s
First record of yodeling
1984
Klingon language invented for a Star Trek movie
c. late 1400s
Modern English first appears
c. early 2000s
Marie Wilcox works to save the Wukchumni language

FUTURE
Text words that have made their way to conversation

TWO

SPEAK UP

Since we don't know when humans first began to speak, it's also nearly impossible to figure out what the first language might have been. Consider this. There are now nearly 7,000 languages spoken around the world today. Many of them have a common ancestor. Like humans, they're related to each other. So is it possible that all our languages sprang from one early prehistoric language? Some language experts, or ***linguists***, say it is. Others are not so sure.

In the 1880s a Polish doctor named Ludwik Zamenhof thought it would be a great idea to create one common language that could be spoken by everyone around the world. He envisioned it as a second language rather than one that would replace a person's original language. Zamenhof called this international language Esperanto, and it was a blend of European languages. While it didn't take off quite as he'd hoped, it's estimated that as many as two million people worldwide speak Esperanto today.

On the Move

If one language did start it all, where and when did that happen? We have to get to know our ancient ancestors first to figure that out. That brings us to East Africa about 300,000 years ago. Most scientists believe that our early relatives, known as ***Homo sapiens***, lived here. At some point these family members of ours began to speak instead of using only gestures and sounds. Some linguists agree with George Poulos, whom we met in the previous chapter, and believe this early language happened gradually over tens of thousands of years. But, as seems to be the case with this topic, others disagree. They suggest language developed more quickly—over a few thousand years—once humans got started. Either way, it's believed our ancestors began to ***migrate***, or move, out of Africa about 80,000 years ago. And as they traveled to Asia, Europe and the Americas, they brought their language or languages along with them.

Not One and Done

Whether or not one language started it all, it's clear that humans have mastered the art of chitchatting. But why do we have so many languages? The answer is one you've heard before: scientists can't say for sure! It may be due to the fact that as humans migrated from Africa, they ended up in different spots around the globe. Each place had its own landscape and challenges. For instance, a group might have made its home in a mountainous region, and another may have settled in a forested area. Each group's words began to evolve as they communicated about their unique environment, food and circumstances. And, over time, new languages were formed. As people continued to migrate to different corners of the world, there was even more opportunity for new languages to form.

Languages have also grown and changed as a result of invasions or war. For example, the early form of English evolved after the Anglo-Saxons—a group of people from northern Europe—invaded and conquered Britain in the fifth century. The Anglo-Saxons had their own language, and it ended up becoming the basis of English. (Prior to this, the people of Britain spoke Celtic languages, which are similar to today's Scottish Gaelic or Welsh.) In the years that followed, the English language developed further after the Vikings invaded parts of England and brought their own language along with them. Modern English as we know it began to appear around the late 1400s. Today English is spoken as a first language by nearly 400 million people around the planet.

Languages are often grouped in families. Those that are on the same family tree descended from a common language. For example, the Indo-European family includes languages such as English, Russian and Hindi-Urdu. They're spoken by over three billion people around the world. And the languages in the Sino-Tibetan family include Mandarin, Tibetan and Burmese. About 1.5 billion people speak these languages.

APPROACH OF THE DANISH FLEET.

Danish Vikings sailed the seas and reached Britain throughout the 8th to 11th centuries. They came ashore and raided the British Isles, settling in eastern areas of the country.

DUNCAN1890/GETTY IMAGES

In Danger

Regardless of the reasons for it, humans have developed thousands of languages. Some, like Mandarin, have millions of speakers. Others have only a handful. Take Łingít. This language is spoken by just a few hundred Łingít people in southeast Alaska, parts of northern British Columbia and southern Yukon. In the past, European colonizers forced this community, and other Indigenous communities, to relinquish their beliefs, as well as their languages. When a language has so few speakers, it's considered endangered. Just like plants and animals that are classified as endangered species, an endangered language faces the possibility of becoming extinct in the near future. And we're not talking about one or two languages. According to the United Nations, at least 50 percent of today's spoken languages will become extinct or seriously endangered within the next 75 years.

STOLEN LANGUAGES

Languages disappear for a number of reasons. If we step back in time, we can track the destruction of Indigenous languages in North America to the genocide that Indigenous Peoples experienced with the arrival of Europeans to the Americas. Beginning in the 1400s, Europeans crossed the ocean to colonize lands, building settlements in places that were new to them. These settlers brought diseases that wiped out entire Indigenous communities and, with them, their languages. Sometimes the reason for the loss of language was even more deliberate. These same settlers demanded that Indigenous Peoples reject their own beliefs and culture to embrace European values, forbidding them to speak their own languages. The European settler governments and Christian religious organizations removed children from their families, sending them to residential schools. Here they were forced to speak English or French and punished for using their own languages. This contributed to the loss of languages like Eyak and Myaamiaataweenki. This went on for hundreds of years. As a result, many Indigenous languages—likely a few hundred—became what's called *sleeping languages*. That means some were lost forever. While some of these Indigenous languages are being spoken again, some are not due to a lack of recorded information about the language.

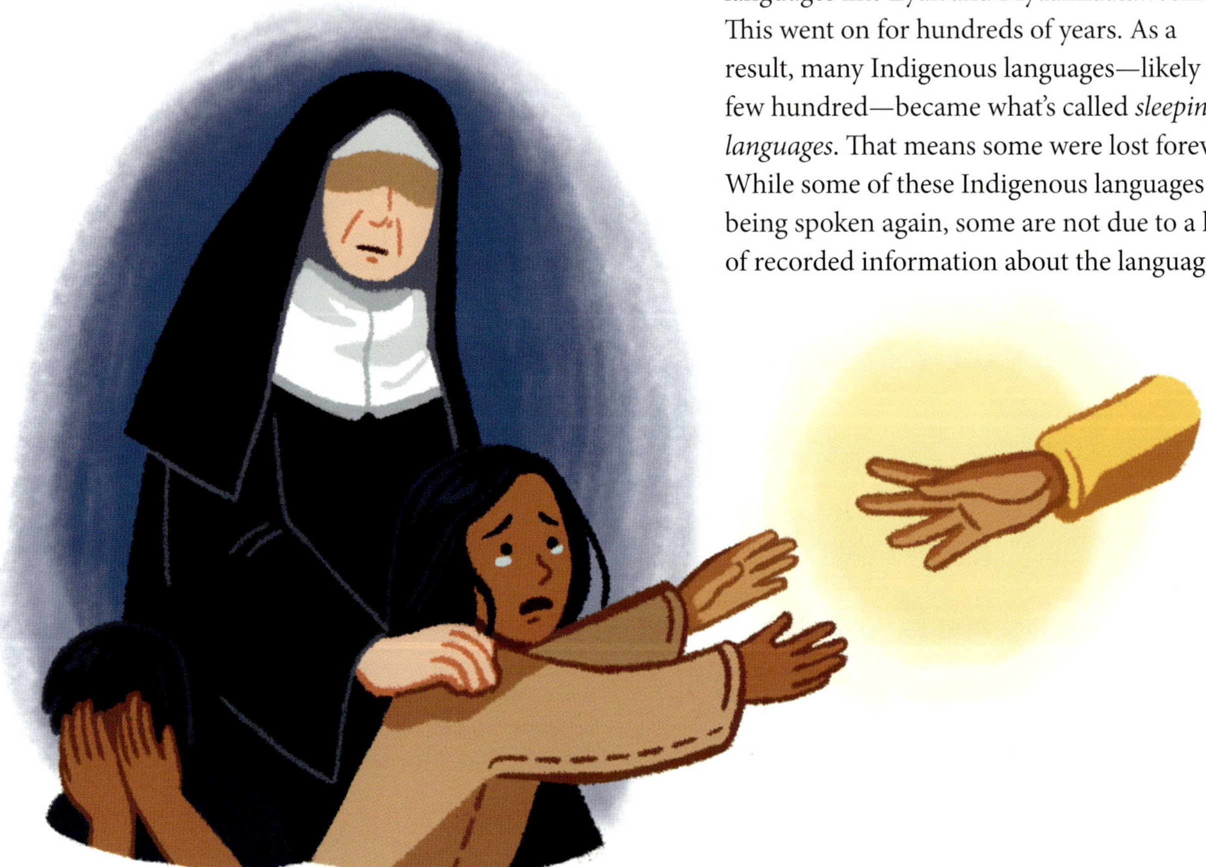

Marie Wilcox was the last fluent speaker of the Indigenous language called Wukchumni. She spent two decades creating a dictionary of the language, even including sound recordings of each word. Wilcox also taught the language in classes to people in her community.
TOMMY LEE KREGER/WIKIMEDIA COMMONS/ CC BY 2.0 DEED

Back from the Brink

So why does it matter if a language disappears? A language is a crucial part of the history and culture of those who speak it. When one goes extinct, we lose knowledge about that culture and the heritage of the people who spoke it. In the same way that we work to protect endangered species around the planet, linguists and historians say we must protect languages.

Some people dedicate themselves to making sure a particular language doesn't disappear. Marie Wilcox, for example, made the decision to share and teach her ancestral language, which had been designated a sleeping language. At one point, Wilcox was the only fluent speaker of the Wukchumni language, a dialect of the Tule-Kaweah language. Tule-Kaweah is the language spoken by the Yokuts, Indigenous nations whose traditional territory can be found in Central California near the Tule and Kaweah Rivers. To make sure the language didn't die with her, she spent the last 20 years of her life creating a Wukchumni dictionary. She also recorded the pronunciations of the words. Before she died in 2021, many of her family members, including her grandchildren, had begun learning Wukchumni. Wilcox's efforts to bring her knowledge of her language to her community are inspiring to all who work to learn their own ancestral language.

The Birth of a Language

While there are endangered languages in many corners of the world, there have been a few instances of new languages emerging. Take this example from Nicaragua. During the late 1970s, the Nicaraguan government set up the first public school for deaf kids, and more schools and programs sprung from it. It's important to understand that this was a time when deaf kids rarely met other deaf kids in Nicaragua. They usually stayed close to home, using simple signs to communicate with their family and friends. There was no official sign language used in the country. Now these kids were hanging out with other deaf kids. The only problem was, the new schools didn't teach sign language as a form of communication. Instead they focused on teaching kids how to speak and lip-read Spanish.

This learning proved to be difficult for the deaf students. At one of the large new schools that opened in the 1980s, things began to change. In the students' free time—in the schoolyard or the bus ride to and from school—they began to sign to each other using the different gestures they used at home. Over the course of the next few years, the students standardized these gestures, and their sign language grew and got more complicated, with its own grammar and words and phrases. New students learned the language from others as they arrived at the school, helping the language thrive and grow.

When the school's administration saw what was happening, they invited a linguist named Judy Kegl to visit. She observed the students and confirmed that the kids had created their own sign language—now known as Nicaraguan Sign Language. In 1986 she declared that it was the birth of a new language. It's believed to be the first time that anyone has witnessed a language starting from scratch.

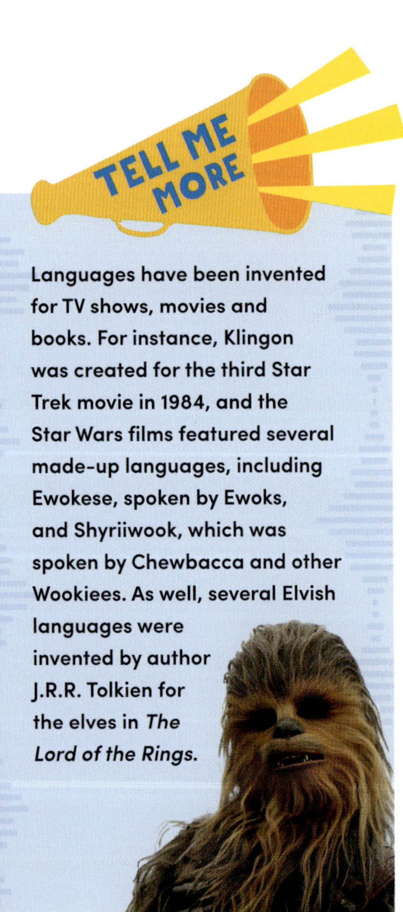

Languages have been invented for TV shows, movies and books. For instance, Klingon was created for the third Star Trek movie in 1984, and the Star Wars films featured several made-up languages, including Ewokese, spoken by Ewoks, and Shyriiwook, which was spoken by Chewbacca and other Wookiees. As well, several Elvish languages were invented by author J.R.R. Tolkien for the elves in *The Lord of the Rings*.

TRISTAN FEWINGS/GETTY IMAGES

TALK • ABOUT • IT

Communication can take many forms. Here are some unusual languages used to stay in touch.

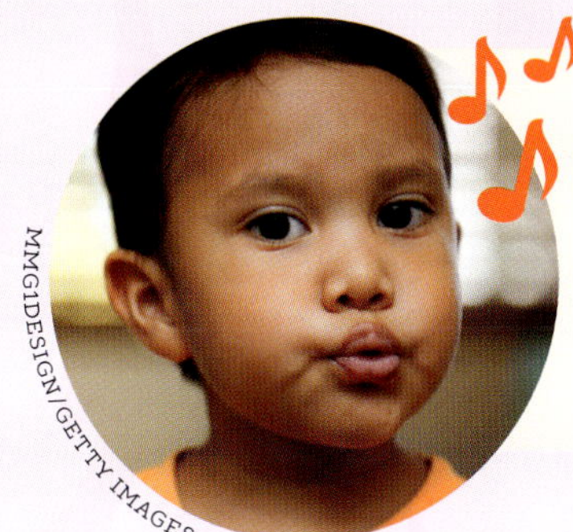

MMGIDESIGN/GETTY IMAGES

Whistling: This rare language is found in several places around the world, including in Turkey, Mexico and some Inuit communities. Those who use a whistling language aren't whistling a tune, though. They "speak" in whistles that are based on their spoken language. Whistling is generally used in forested or mountainous areas because it allows people to communicate over long distances. After all, a loud series of whistles travels farther than speaking or yelling does.

YODEL-AY-EEE-OO

SANDRA FOYT/SHUTTERSTOCK.COM

Yodeling: You've probably heard yodeling at some point. It's a form of singing in which the singer repeatedly switches between their regular voice and a higher pitch. But from at least the 1500s, this lyrical language was used to communicate in the Swiss Alps. Farmers yodeled in the mountains to round up their cows and goats. And a farmer might yodel to communicate with other farmer in a village across the valley. While most people associate yodeling with Switzerland, some experts suggest it originated in Africa about 10,000 years ago.

TTYL
LOL
HBU

RICHARD DRURY/GETTY IMAGES

Textese: *You* might "speak" this language. It first appeared on the scene in the late 1990s. And it's a written language—typed language may be more accurate—that's used for sending messages on smartphones. Textese allows a speaker to abbreviate, or shorten, words in their message. For instance, in English you might type *4ever* instead of *forever*. Or you might include an *LOL* in your message rather than typing *laugh out loud*.

Who's the best baby in the world?

SOLSTOCK/GETTY IMAGES

Parentese: Studies have found that parents speak to their babies in a special way that's different from how they speak to adults. They're not just *goo-goo, gaa-gaa* sounds. This language, called parentese, has an almost musical and exaggerated tone that sounds higher than the mom's or dad's regular speaking voice. Experts have found that this switch to parentese happens with parents around the world and in a variety of spoken languages. And it's done without thinking about it. Researchers believe this style of speech is a good thing for babies. It gets their attention and also helps improve a baby's language skills, since they are more likely to babble and try to respond to their parent's when they hear it.

TELL ME MORE

In case you're curious about the meaning of those unusual words—*yonks, hornswoggle* and *gadzooks*—here's what they mean. *Yonks* means "a very long time," *hornswoggle* means "to trick" and *gadzooks* is an expression you use when you're surprised or shocked.

Time for a Change

Languages tend to change over time regardless of how old they are. Take English, for example. Even though there are already roughly one million words, humans constantly create new words, causing the language to grow. In fact, an American company that tracks the English language says about 5,400 new words are created each year. So how does that happen? Haven't we already found a way to say everything we want with the words we already have? Apparently not. A professor at the University of Toronto named Marcel Danesi studies language and has a few thoughts on our ever-expanding ***vocabulary***. For one thing, he explains, new ideas and objects come about all the time, and we're left needing words to describe them. An example he uses is the utensil that combines a spoon with the tines of a fork, a new type of cutlery that led to the creation of the word *spork*.

And sometimes, Danesi points out, the meaning of a word changes from how it was originally used. Take the word *sick*. During the 1980s people began using this word to mean "cool" or "awesome" rather than "ill." And this usage caught on, especially among skateboarders and snowboarders. Today it's still used by people to say something's cool. And if you look in the dictionary, you'll find the ***slang*** definition of it included with the standard definitions. But who knows how long people will use *sick* this way? As Danesi points out, some words remain in our conversations for centuries, while others eventually disappear. Have you ever heard the words *yonks, hornswoggle* or *gadzooks*? Use of these once widely known words has dropped off. So who's to say which words will fade away next?

It's common for people to send text messages from their smartphones at least a few times a day. Some smartphones limit a text message to 160 characters, including letters, numbers, spaces and punctuation.
MAYUR KAKADE/GETTY IMAGES

Communication IRL

In today's world of instant communication, texting has had an impact on our spoken language too. Some of the abbreviations we use in our texts have found their way from our smartphones into our everyday conversations. Two of the most popular—LOL and OMG—have been in use since the 1990s, when ***text messaging*** came on the scene. If you'd been around even 20 years ago, you likely wouldn't have imagined language changing in this way.

Most of us say things like *um, uh, like* or *you know* in our conversations. These are known as filler words, and every language has them. We tend to use them to fill a pause while we're thinking about what to say next. And though it might not seem like it, they have a purpose. Linguists say filler words help us arrange our thoughts as we're speaking. And they also give other people time to take in what we're saying. Some people believe we should avoid filler words because they can become distracting and interfere with communication. But linguists argue these words are an element of language, and if we banish *um* or *like*, we'll just find other words to replace them as we speak.

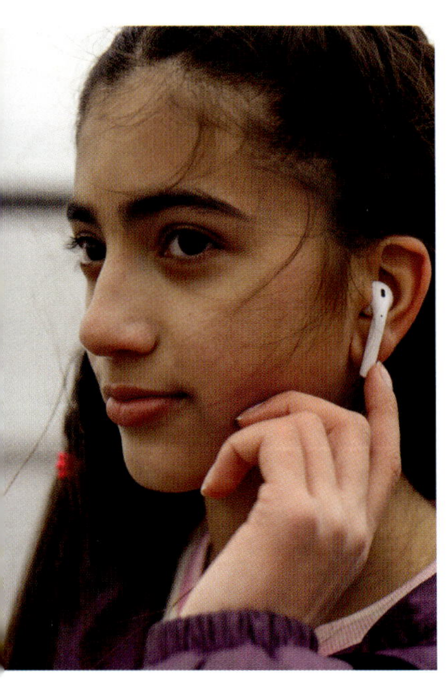

Besides being used as a listening device, some earbuds can translate languages for the wearer.
SOLSTOCK/GETTY IMAGES

IS TECH FOR EVERYONE?

Experts say that more changes in our language are likely to come as new technologies arrive. Of course, without knowing what future tech will be like, we don't know what new forms of language might evolve. But it's concerning that newer technology tends to understand or include only a few of the world's languages, with English being one of the main ones. That's great if you're an English speaker, but what about those who communicate in one of the other nearly 7,000 languages on the planet? Will they be left out when it comes to using the latest cutting-edge tech?

ALL AROUND THE WORLD

While certain new technology seems to be leaving some of us behind, some people are working toward breaking down language barriers and helping humans communicate more easily with one another. For instance, in 2022, a set of earbuds were unveiled that can translate a number of languages almost instantly. Here's how they work. When you speak, the earbuds translate your words into another language. Then they are read aloud by an app on your phone, so the person you're speaking with can hear them. And if that person responds in a different language, the earbuds translate and send the translation straight through your earbuds so you understand. This device is a glimpse of what may be to come—that is, technology that can translate conversations with anyone you meet. Of course, translating each and every language is a huge undertaking. But just imagine what it would mean for human communication if we could connect with someone regardless of where we are in the world and no matter the language they speak.

TALK • ABOUT • IT

There are no creatures in the animal kingdom that can communicate by speaking like we do. They don't have the voice box and brain function that allow it. But they do have ways of communicating with others in their species. Here are a few examples.

Honeybees: To communicate, bees perform a "waggle dance." After a bee finds a food source, it flies back to the hive and does this dance by shaking its abdomen and dancing in a figure-eight pattern. These dance moves tell the other bees exactly where to find the flower that will provide some good eats!

Peacocks: It was once thought that peacocks display their flashy tails to attract females, called peahens. But a study by two scientists at the University of Manitoba discovered that they also use their colorful tails to communicate with other peacocks. They shake their tails to create a low, rumbling sound that can't be heard by humans. This sound tells peahens that a male is looking for a mate—and it warns other males to steer clear of its territory.

Prairie dogs: These small mammals make a variety of sounds to stay in touch, including barks, squeaks and chirps. Biologists say each of these sounds has its own meaning. And while each call is less than one second long, it gets the point across. For instance, one call might warn the colony to beware of an approaching predator, and another may allow a mom to tell her young to follow her.

Trees: Okay, so trees aren't animals. But since they are part of the natural world, it seems fitting to mention that they also communicate. The roots of trees contain plantlike organisms called fungi. Fungi provide the nutrients needed for trees to survive. Nearby trees are linked together underground by a network of fungi. And this network can be used to send chemical signals to each other to communicate about dangers such as disease, drought or insect threats.

c.1970s
GPS technology developed
HELLO
c. 3000 BCE
Lighthouses first used to guide ships
c.1915
Invention of skywriting
FUTURE
Conversation with AI
?

THREE

SPREAD THE WORD

Even though language was well on its way to becoming the easiest method for humans to stay in touch, sometimes circumstances meant we needed other ways to communicate. That is, methods that were nonverbal—or didn't use words—and went beyond gestures. This was especially true when we wanted to connect from a distance. Remember, there were no telephones, no computers and no internet in centuries past! So when we needed to pass along information, whether it was about possible threats or to provide directions from afar, we had to find a way. Since humans are ever creative, we discovered methods for keeping the lines of communication open whether we were near or far apart.

1914
Vatican announces new pope with white smoke signal

Smoke signals are only used in a few ways today. When a new pope is elected in the Catholic Church, white smoke billows from the chimney of the Sistine Chapel in Rome to announce that a decision has been made. And smoke signals are also used by armies, who set off smoke grenades on the ground to show a helicopter where it can land safely.

Up in Smoke

The earliest forms of long-distance communication took some work to understand. People received messages, but they had to know how to decipher them. Smoke signals were one of the first methods of communication used over distances, and they were adopted by several communities.

Ancient China: Smoke signals were used by soldiers stationed atop the Great Wall of China—one of the largest human-made structures in history—beginning around 300 BCE. This wall was built as a way for emperors to protect their land from enemies. Watchtowers were placed along the winding wall so Chinese soldiers could stand on guard. If they noticed enemies approaching, they lit a fire using twigs, dried grasses or even wolf dung. The columns of smoke from the fire signaled to soldiers in watchtowers farther away that rival troops were coming and it was time to prepare for battle. The messages were transmitted quickly over hundreds of miles.

Skywriting is usually done by one aircraft. Its message in the sky lasts for about 10 minutes on average.
29BUCUK/SHUTTERSTOCK.COM

North American Indigenous Peoples: It's been a common stereotype throughout the past two centuries that all Indigenous groups in North America once used smoke signals to communicate. But, according to experts, this is not the case. Only a few, including the Navajo and Apache, relied on them. Several hundred years ago, these signals were used mainly for the same reason as the ancient Chinese—to warn of approaching enemies. An individual would stand atop a hill and create a fire with dried grasses, sending billowing smoke into the sky.

South American Indigenous Peoples: The Yahgan People live on the southernmost tip of South America. In the past they often sent messages to other members of the community using smoke signals, especially about the location of food. For example, if a whale washed ashore, this hunter-gatherer community wanted to be sure the meat didn't decay and go to waste. So archaeologists say whoever came upon the creature sent up smoke signals to notify others in the community to come and gather some meat.

Skywriting—forming words in the sky using vapors released from an airplane—dates to World War I, when pilots sent out smoke signals from their planes' exhaust systems. But one pilot, Captain Cyril Turner, took it a step further. In 1922 he realized he could write short ads with this smoke in clear blue skies for companies looking to promote their products to crowds below. His idea took off, and skywriting became a common way to advertise over the next few decades.

Say It with Flames

Where there's smoke, there's fire. And it turns out that huge bonfires were another way people stayed in touch. The Byzantine Empire was a powerful civilization that ruled parts of Europe from about 330 to 1453. It built a series of brick towers miles apart on hilltops throughout its territory. When an oncoming enemy was spotted, a fire was lit atop a nearby tower. Soon enough a soldier in the next tower over would see the flames and light his own signal fire. This continued down the line of towers, which stretched across an extensive area measuring 450 miles (720 kilometers). The system worked so well that the message of danger could be transmitted from one end of the empire to the other in about an hour.

LIGHT THE WAY

Fire has also been used to communicate with sailors to keep them safe during their travels. This was done using lighthouses. Standing along shorelines or even out on reefs in the sea, lighthouses are designed to shine a light that guides boats and ships safely along coastlines and into harbors. They've been around since at least the time of the ancient Egyptians, or about 5,000 years ago. Early lighthouses used open fires in their domes as a beacon to help sailors ***navigate*** rocky shorelines. Eventually oil lamps were set up at the top of lighthouses, and a mirror was used to reflect the light of their flame out to those at sea. It wasn't always the brightest light, but it did provide some help with navigation.

In the early 1820s a French physicist named Augustin-Jean Fresnel invented a special lens—a piece of curved glass that bends light. It focused the light from a lamp into a strong beam that could be seen by seafarers who were miles out at sea, making it easier for them to determine the direction of land and keep them safely on course. Most of today's lighthouses are powered by electricity or solar energy. But with the availability of other guiding tools, like the global positioning system (GPS)—a system that can detect the location of something on Earth—lighthouses aren't relied on nearly as much by sailors as they were in past centuries.

The Lighthouse of Alexandria was built by the ancient Egyptians in the third century BCE. It stood in the harbor of Alexandria, the capital city of Egypt at the time. Today it's considered one of the Seven Wonders of the Ancient World.

MIKROMAN6/GETTY IMAGES

The Cabo Vilán lighthouse is on the shores of the west coast of Spain. It was built in 1896 after a British ship sailed into the rocks along the coastline during a storm, causing the deaths of over 170 sailors.

CARLOS FERNANDEZ/GETTY IMAGES

A beacon is designed to attract attention to a particular area. Take this modern-day beacon found on a hill in Scotland. It was lit to mark important occasions during the reign of Queen Elizabeth II.

TALK • ABOUT • IT

Sometimes nature has given humans a helping hand in communication. Check out these methods that relied on the natural world to help send messages.

Sun signals: The Minoans, a civilization that lived on the Greek island of Crete from about 3000 BCE, turned to the sun to communicate. They relied on a signaling method called ***heliographic messaging***. That's a fancy way of saying they used shiny silver and bronze plates to flash rays of sunlight at each other. By reflecting the sun's rays, they could send coded messages to people on other parts of the island. The Ponca nations, who live in the midwestern United States, once used sheets of a shiny mineral called mica to reflect the sun and pass along hunting messages to others in their community.

Homing pigeons: These birds have been used to carry messages for thousands of years. You could call them some of the world's earliest postal carriers! Homing pigeons have a knack for finding their way home, so a person would attach their message to a pigeon's leg and send it on its way to deliver news. The ancient Greeks used pigeons to announce events like the Olympic Games and their results. And Genghis Khan, a warrior who built a huge empire from China to Eastern Europe in the 1200s, built an entire communication system using pigeons to carry messages throughout the land. Homing pigeons were also used during both World War I and II to quickly deliver crucial information between the soldiers on the front lines and those back at a military base.

Beat It

Even a musical instrument can be used to communicate. Take a drum known as the dùndún, or, more commonly, the talking drum. It began to be used in West Africa likely as early as the year 600. While we typically think of drumming as a musical expression, this hourglass-shaped drum can also be used to imitate the sound of human speech, specifically an African language called Yoruba, when played in a particular rhythm. The talking drum was used as a tool for communication, with skilled drummers sending messages to drummers in other villages located miles away. These drummers then relayed the information to those in their villages, making it a quick way to spread news and information.

Interestingly, the talking drum is thought to have been used by West Africans for communication during the transatlantic slave trade, which began beginning in the early 1500s and saw Black Africans captured by Europeans, sold into slavery and transported to colonies across the ocean. When African villagers saw European enslavers approaching, they drummed out warning messages on the dùndún so that people in surrounding villages could escape. And during the 1700s, drums were banned by owners of enslaved people in North America because they feared the people they enslaved would use them to communicate and fight against their enslavement. Today the drum is usually played for musical expression.

Time for some tunes! Drummers make music on traditional African drums while walking through a Nigerian village.

Sometimes people rely on their voice to make their point. In medieval England, for instance, it was common to find a person called a town crier on the streets. They had one job: to make public announcements for the monarchy by loudly crying out the latest news or proclamations as they rang a bell. Information was shared this way because most people of the time couldn't read.

BRYAN LEDGAR/WIKIMEDIA COMMONS/ CC BY 2.0 DEED

THE LOUDER THE BETTER

Another object we associate with music, the horn, was also used by humans to communicate over long distances. In many ancient cultures, people transformed horns from creatures such as cattle, buffalo and antelopes by hollowing them out. Then someone could blow into the end to create a loud sound. Oftentimes blowing the horn signified the start of a celebration. But there were also times when a horn was used to warn of an approaching enemy.

Eventually the cone-like shape of the horn inspired a speaking instrument called a megaphone, which could be used to ***amplify*** (increase the loudness of) a voice. This made sure a speaker's words were loud enough to be heard by many people in an area. The history of this invention is sketchy. Two different people are credited with inventing the megaphone in the late 1600s, both an English mathematician and a German scholar.

HELLO OUT THERE

That said, there is evidence that megaphones of different types have been used for communication for centuries in places around the world. For example, Iscouakité, the leader of the Odawa Nation, is said to have used a megaphone-like tube made of birchbark in the late 1600s.

And some experts believe a version of the megaphone was used by the ancient Greeks. This civilization often put on plays in huge outdoor theaters, with actors wearing masks so an audience could distinguish one character from another. These audiences were massive, some having upward of 10,000 people! Experts think the masks had small built-in megaphones around the mouth openings to amplify the actors' voices for the people in the seats farthest from the stage.

Can you hear me? A handheld megaphone is shaped like a cone. It helps make your voice louder and directs it toward people in the distance.

FG TRADE/GETTY IMAGES

ANDRAS CSONTOS/DREAMSTIME.COM

LAURENBERGSTROM/GETTY IMAGES

In the early 1900s a new invention drove on to the scene to make communication easier on the road—the car horn. Before this time, drivers often used bells or whistles to let pedestrians know they were near. Today we often think that people lay on the horn to express their frustration with another driver. But researchers who have studied horn honking say that in other places around the world, drivers often use car horns as a language all its own. For instance, a certain series of long and short beeps on the horn might be used to greet a friend who's walking along the sidewalk.

Beeps might also help celebrate a happy occasion or even be a way to say "I love you" to a fellow driver. Seriously! In Cairo, Egypt, there's a particular series of horn beeps that relays this message!

VITEEVATIY/GETTY IMAGES

I'm Here for You

Today a voice of a different sort has become a common part of our daily lives. And it's one that isn't even real. Enter the voice assistant. These voice-activated devices respond to our questions and commands. We can ask them to perform tasks—play our favorite tunes, take photos for us or provide us with the weather forecast. They are part of special computer programs that are designed to listen, recognize a human voice and communicate with users to help out. Voice assistants do this using artificial intelligence (AI)—that's the ability of a computer to process and learn, imitating intelligent human behavior. Voice assistants are found in items like smart speakers, watches, phones and tablets. You may be familiar with two common voice assistants, Alexa and Siri, but Audrey was the first, back in 1952. Audrey could recognize a human voice speaking the digits zero through nine, so it could be used to dial a telephone hands-free.

Since voice assistants aren't real people, we can't have a proper back-and-forth conversation with them. But could that happen in the future? Will we be able to chitchat with our voice assistants? Experts aren't convinced. One of the big reasons is that computers are built to process information, not think and feel like humans do. So having a genuine conversation with a voice assistant seems unlikely. That said, it's expected they'll begin to help us out in new ways in the future. They might one day make helpful suggestions in our daily life instead of waiting around for commands from us. For instance, a voice assistant that's found in a car might notice when our vehicle's battery is running low and suggest it's time for a charge.

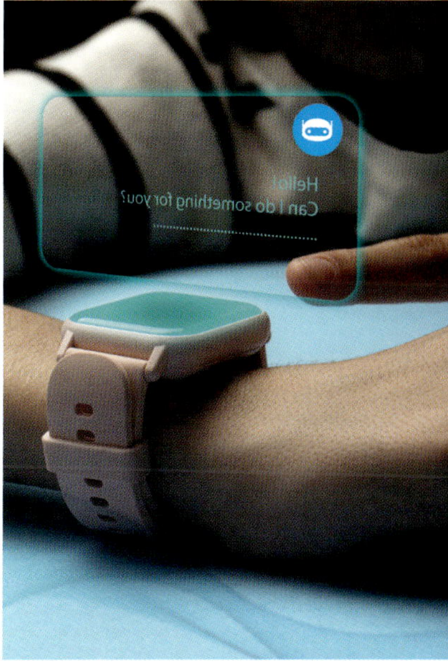

A smartwatch is a wearable computer device. Today's smartwatches do more than tell the time. They can also make phone calls, send emails, tell you the weather or play music. And in the future, who knows what else these devices might do!

FRANCESCO CARTA FOTOGRAFO/ GETTY IMAGES

c. 400 BCE
Persian Empire begins using organized mail system
c. 1996
Port Lockroy post office opens
c. 3500 BCE
Cuneiform system of writing invented
1824
Louis Braille invents braille

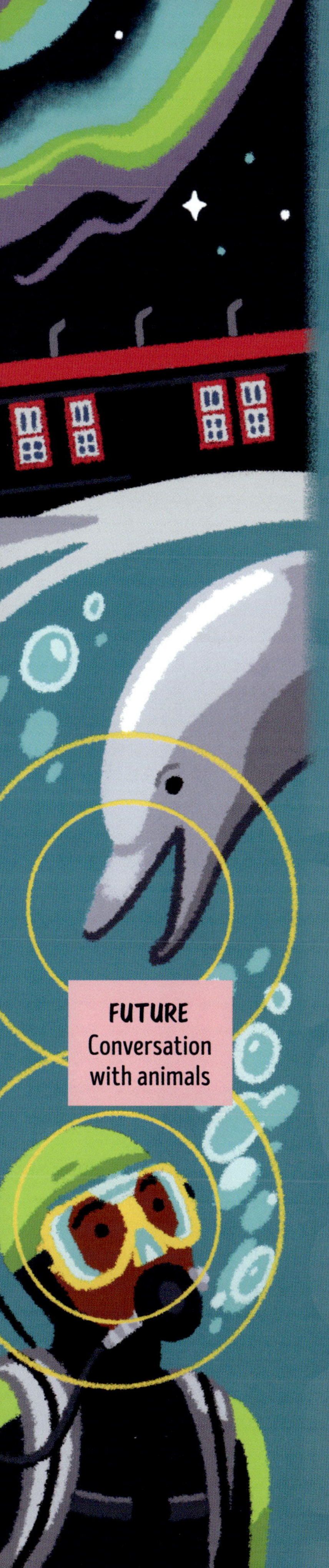

FOUR

GOING THE DISTANCE

One of the most important advances in our ability to communicate was the development of writing. It provided a physical way to communicate back and forth. Writing was especially helpful for trading and as people migrated to new places. While it was first used for practical purposes, writing evolved to become a way we could express ourselves creatively. So when and where did writing begin? And how did it evolve? Let's see what scholars have come to learn.

What's old is new again. Today we refer to the portable electronic computers we use as tablets. Interestingly, our ancient ancestors also used tablets. But theirs were flat slabs of clay, stone or wood!

The Write Stuff

Around 3500 BCE, the ancient Sumerians—one of the oldest civilizations, which emerged in the Middle East—created the earliest known system of writing. Called cuneiform (*say: kyoo-nee-uh-form*), it featured symbols pressed into clay tablets. The system likely came about for trading purposes. People wanted to keep track of what they'd bought and sold. But at the time, very few people could read and write this language system—only about 10 percent of the population. Those who knew the system were called ***scribes***. And they studied for years to perfect the art of writing cuneiform.

Not long after the Sumerians began writing, the ancient Egyptians followed. Their writing system was called ***hieroglyphics***, and it used thousands of pictures and symbols to represent their language. Instead of clay tablets, they wrote on papyrus, a paperlike material that could be rolled into scrolls. And, as with the Sumerians, only an educated few could read and write hieroglyphics.

Unlike the pencils we use today, early pencils were more like paintbrushes. Each one was made of a hollow wooden tube filled with animal hairs. The modern pencil was invented in the 1600s.
THEPALMER/GETTY IMAGES

The Egyptians used hieroglyphics to carve prayers on tombs as a way to help pharaohs have a safe passage to the afterlife.
B.S.P.I./GETTY IMAGES

Back to the Future?

Today many people have noticed the similarities between ***emojis***—those digital symbols we use on our phones and tablets—and hieroglyphics. The term *emoji* comes from the Japanese language, in which *e* means "picture" and *moji* means "character." And while at first glance we might think emojis are a modern version of the ancient Egyptians' hieroglyphics, they're actually quite different. An emoji is what's known as a pictogram, meaning it's a picture that resembles the emotion or object it represents. But hieroglyphics do much more than that. The pictures in this writing system represent words, phrases and sounds. Moreover, a hieroglyphic character can have a number of meanings. So hieroglyphics are more complex than emojis.

Are you happy or sad? Emojis help us express ourselves without using words.
MARIZZA/GETTY IMAGES

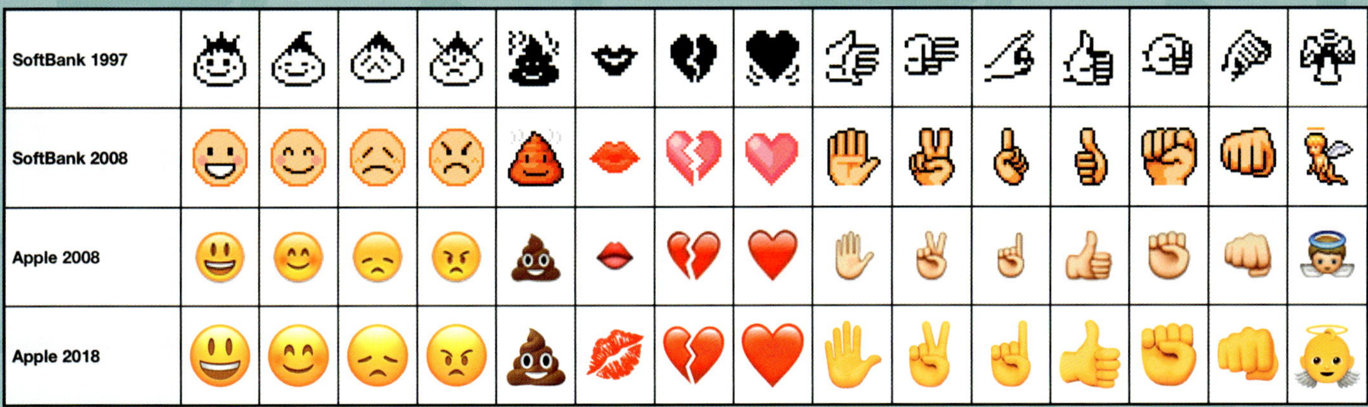

Take a quick look at the emojis above and you'll see how their designs have evolved since they first appeared in the late 1990s.

BLOG.EMOJIPEDIA.ORG

SAY IT WITH SMILEY FACES

The emoji has been around since the late 1990s, but the use of it became more commonplace in about 2010, when an emoji keyboard arrived on smartphones. Today many of us use emojis to communicate. In fact, upward of six billion emojis are sent every single day! And the most popular? The face with tears of joy, which means laughter or extreme happiness.

It might seem that emojis are simply fun symbols to include in our text messages. But our brain says otherwise. Scientists have found that the region in the brain that recognizes faces perceives emojis as if they are real faces with emotions. So if your friend sends a smiling emoji in a text, your brain processes it the same as if you were seeing a smiling human face. That means emojis can actually help us better connect with our pals. We get a sense of the emotions our friends are feeling similar to if we were having face-to-face conversations.

Some say emojis may be the world's only universal language—that is, one that everyone understands regardless of their spoken language. Experts suggest that due to the popularity of emojis, we'll likely continue to see new ones popping up. There are currently over 3,500 different emojis. That sounds like plenty, but there are lots of objects, including cultural symbols and foods and drinks from around that world, that could find their way onto an emoji keyboard.

As technology has advanced, we've seen the arrival of a different type of emoji—the sticker. Stickers are cartoonish illustrations of characters—sometimes meant to resemble people's own faces—that are usually bigger than emojis and can be "stuck" into text messages to express an idea or feeling. Their popularity has increased in the past few years, and some think there may come a time when these stickers will replace common emojis altogether.

The ABCs

Writing continued to evolve over the centuries. Some civilizations moved toward using a set of letters for different sounds that could be arranged to write the words of a particular language. That's how we came to the alphabetic writing used in the English seen on these pages. The alphabet itself wasn't invented—it evolved over time.

Historians say that around 1600 BCE, a group of people who lived in what is now the Middle East adapted the most common hieroglyphics and came up with an alphabet of 22 symbols. Since it focused on a few symbols, rather than the thousands used in the hieroglyphic system, it was easier for merchants and sailors to use as they traveled and traded with other civilizations. By about 1000 BCE, this writing system had spread to Greece, where it was tweaked again. Eventually this Greek alphabet led to the development of the Latin alphabet, which led to the English, Spanish and French alphabets. All this is to say that, while it took a few thousand years, our alphabet descended from ancient Egyptian hieroglyphs.

TELL ME MORE

In the early 1800s, a French inventor named Louis Braille developed a system of raised dots, or bumps, that allows people with visual impairments to read and write. Named after him, braille is read by lightly touching the dots with one's fingertips, moving along from left to right. There are 63 dot patterns that represent letters, numbers and punctuation.

ALLE12/GETTY IMAGES

There are over 700 coding languages for writing computer programs. A few of the most common are JavaScript, Python and Go.
KAZ_C/GETTY IMAGES

Computer Talk

There are many other writing systems around the world, and we're not quite done coming up with new ones. As technology has evolved, we've had to develop written languages that allow humans to communicate with computers. Called coding languages, they help us tell computers what we want them to do. And while coding languages look like nothing but a hodgepodge of letters, numbers and symbols, they give computers step-by-step instructions on how to perform specific tasks. These languages are written by programmers, and they are used for computers of all kinds. Take your gaming consoles, for example. They rely on a coding language that makes the graphics, sounds and controls in your game work properly. And even cars have a computer on board that follows instructions. Coding tells the car how to operate features like its brakes, airbags and alarm system.

TELL ME MORE

Scientists in a field of study called digital bioacoustics are currently working on a way to communicate with something else we're all familiar with—animals! They've placed tiny gadgets that record sounds all around the world, from the tundra to the rainforests. These recorders capture sounds 24-7. Then computers try to detect patterns in the sounds the animals are making. In one instance, a research team analyzed thousands of sounds made by fruit bats. And they figured out what some of their noises mean. Some are made by the bats as they argue over food with other bats. Others are made by mom bats "talking" to their young. The experts say one day we may use this research to "speak" the language of a variety of species!

Pass it on! When we whisper, we squeeze our vocal cords together tightly so they don't vibrate. This helps us speak softly so our conversation isn't overheard.
ROB LEWINE/GETTY IMAGES

Make a Run for It

With written language still something only scribes could do, ancient peoples often sent messages to others using the spoken word. ***Couriers*** traveled on horseback, or even ran on foot, to relay verbal information over long distances. Even when many other cultures had turned to written messages, the Incas—a civilization that ruled parts of South America beginning in the 1100s—relied on a special group of messengers to deliver official government verbal communications throughout the empire. The Inca didn't have a writing system, so young fit men known as chaskis were tasked with memorizing messages and then passing them along verbally. They did this in a relay system, racing for long distances on the roads that had been built across the mountainous terrain. One chaski would repeat the message to another runner, who carried on and passed it along to another chaski, who did the same. In fact, it might take 25 messengers to successfully relay one verbal note. But in just one day, chaskis could transmit a message over a couple hundred miles.

TALK • ABOUT • IT

Sometimes a message was so secret that a sender had to find a way to pass it along on the sly. In ancient times that led to the practice of *steganography*—hiding messages within or on top of ordinary things that are not secret. Here are a few examples of some sneaky ways once used to share information.

Tattoo you: One of the first instances of steganography dates back to the time of the ancient Greeks. Histiaeus, a ruler in Greece during the late sixth century BCE, wanted to overthrow the king of the Persian Empire. To start an uprising, he sent a secret message to his allies...under a messenger's hair. First he had the messenger shave his head. Then the message was tattooed on his scalp. Ouch. From there Histiaeus had to wait for the messenger's hair to grow back before sending him on his way. When he reached his destination, the messenger's head was shaved to reveal the top-secret communication. All this made for a *very*, *very* slow secret delivery!

Save it for later: In ancient China, royal messengers carried secret messages *inside* their bodies. A message was written on a small piece of silk, which was then crumpled into a ball and coated with wax. After that the messenger swallowed the silk ball. At this point, there was only one way to deliver the note. Any guesses? Hold on to your lunch. The messenger had to poop it out!

Invisible ink: A Roman scholar named Pliny the Elder lived in the first century. And he discovered that the milky sap found inside a plant called tithymalus could be used to make invisible ink. A message was written with the sap, and when the sap ***evaporated***, the note could no longer be seen. But there was a trick to make it return. If you sprinkled warm ashes over the message, the dried sap would char and turn brown. And presto, the message reappeared!

Special delivery! Mail usually arrives in a timely fashion. But according to Guinness World Records, the longest postal delay was 89 years. In 2008 a British woman finally received a letter that had been sent to her in 1919!
SDI PRODUCTIONS/GETTY IMAGES

TELL ME MORE

In 1653 a Frenchman named Jean-Jacques Renouard de Villayer decided to create a postal system for Paris. He placed mailboxes around the city and offered prepaid envelopes to people. Customers could put their letters in these envelopes and place them in the mailbox to be delivered. Unfortunately, Renouard de Villayer's postal business hit a snag when some people—perhaps messengers afraid they'd lose their jobs—decided to place mice inside the mailboxes. The little rodents chewed up the mail, and with that customers stopped using the service. It was another few hundred years later before a successful postal system eventually delivered mail to citizens throughout France.

You've Got Mail

By 400 BCE a more extensive and organized mail system had arrived on the scene to make for easier communication across large areas of land. In the Persian Empire, which stretched from Greece all the way to India, written messages were sent regularly by emperors and officials. According to historian Lindsay Allen, a message would be written in ink on dried animal skin and in one language—Aramaic. Then the letter was folded up, sealed and sent via a messenger on horseback along the Persian Royal Road, an ancient highway built through the empire. Expert horsemen known as angaros carried, delivered and picked up mail across the vast land. The letters were moved along through a relay system, with an angaro handing off their mail to the next angaro after traveling a certain distance. This system was used only for official government communication. Personal messages had to find their way to their destinations with friends or travelers.

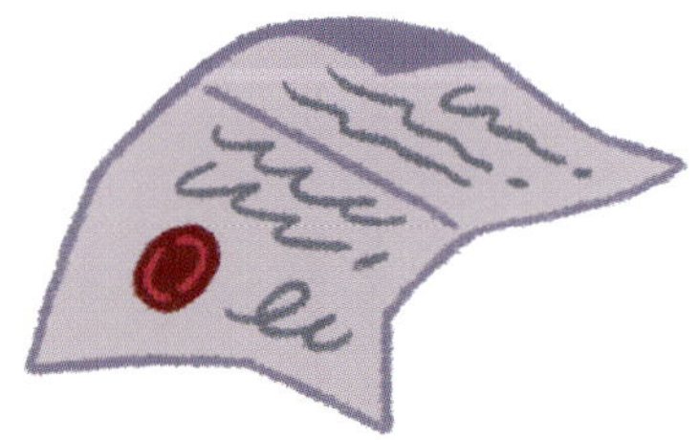

When in Rome

The ancient Romans developed their own postal system, called the cursus publicus, around 20 BCE. At this time the Romans had already established an extensive network of stone roads that stretched 50,000 miles (80,500 kilometers) across the empire. They were built to allow troops to make their way quickly across the realm and to connect cities. But the roadways also made for a fast and efficient way to deliver letters. Couriers on horseback or with horse-drawn mail carts carried important government messages along the empire's roadways. Messages were written on papyrus, animal skin or wax-coated tablets. Along the roads there were stations, called "mutationes," where a messenger could swap out a tired horse for another before hitting the road again.

Put Your Stamp on It

As for our modern postal system, we can trace that back to England in the late 1830s. That's when a British man named Rowland Hill suggested that the sender of a letter should pay for it to be delivered rather than the recipient, as was common at the time. He also came up with the idea of a postage stamp that could be stuck on mail as a form of payment based on the weight of the letter or package. The British government liked Hill's idea so much that his postal system had come into use by 1840. And it soon became the standard in places around the world.

Over the following decades, with the development of trains, trucks and airplanes, the postal system improved and became more efficient. Mail could easily be transported hundreds and eventually thousands of miles a day. Today it's estimated that over 200 billion letters are processed each year around the world. Of course, email has taken over our communication, allowing us to send our messages around the world almost immediately. Consider this. Over 350 billion emails are sent and received *every day* around the world! Not surprisingly, this has led to a drastic reduction in the number of letters heading into mailboxes.

MANUEL ESTEBAN/DREAMSTIME.COM

Tourists often send postcards to friends back home while on vacation. However, some people don't mail postcards. They collect them. The hobby of collecting postcards is called deltiology.

IMGORTHAND/GETTY IMAGES

TALK • ABOUT • IT

Post offices provide a place for people to drop off their mail for delivery. While most are pretty ordinary, a few around the world stand out.

Found in the southwestern Pacific Ocean, the Vanuatu Post is located 10 feet (3 meters) underwater! It's available to divers and snorkelers looking to send a note. Of course, paper mail might get a bit soggy in the sea, so people are provided with special waterproof postcards to drop in the mailbox.

A wooden barrel served as a post office on one of the Galápagos Islands. It was 1793 when a British Royal Navy officer named Captain James Colnett installed the barrel along the sandy shores of Floreana Island for passing sailors looking to mail letters. Sailors dropped their messages in the barrel and other seafarers scooped them up if they were heading in the same direction as the mail. Today there is a replica of the barrel on the island, and tourists can still drop off letters and postcards. If another tourist finds mail destined for a place near where they live, they'll snatch it up and mail it once they get back home. Mail from this post office might not arrive for weeks, months or even years!

People can mail more than letters and packages from a post office on the Hawaiian island of Molokai. The Hoolehua post office offers a Post-a-Nut service: tourists can write a short note on a coconut and have it mailed to just about anywhere in the world. The post office sends out thousands of coconuts each year.

VANUATU POST LIMITED, VANUATUPOST.VU

DANIEL SAMBRAUS/GETTY IMAGES

PASIEKA/GETTY IMAGES

Gentoo penguins waddle around outside this remote post office at Port Lockroy, Antarctica. In fact, it's nicknamed the Penguin Post Office thanks to the penguins who call the area home. This southernmost post office is a popular destination for the tourists traveling on cruise ships around here. They stop during their expeditions to drop off mail so friends and family can receive a delivery all the way from chilly Antarctica.

PASIEKA/GETTY IMAGES

FUTURE
Augmented reality glasses
c.1440s
Modern printing press invented by Gutenberg
1969
World watches on TV as Apollo 11 spacecraft lands on the moon
c.1830s
Morse code invented

1973
Cell phone, known as "the Brick," becomes available to the public

FIVE

TECH TALK

While writing made communication easier for humans, the ability to communicate with one another flourished even more as we developed new technologies. This got started around the 1400s, and communication has evolved at a breakneck speed ever since. Just think. People once sent messages by horseback, which were received days later, while we can reach out to someone on the other side of the world in a matter of moments. So how did we arrive at this point? Follow along as technology makes long-distance human communication instantaneous.

All the News That's Fit to Print

A replica of Johannes Gutenberg's printing press is found in a museum in Germany. Visitors can watch a demonstration of printing done by the replica.
(MAIN) DIEGO GRANDI/DREAMSTIME.COM; (INSET) NYC WANDERER (KEVIN ENG)/ WIKIMEDIA COMMONS/CC BY 2.0 DEED

In the 1440s German inventor Johannes Gutenberg devised the modern printing press. This meant printed pages could be created easily and quickly. Before this, text generally had to be written by hand. And, of course, this took lots of time and effort. With Gutenberg's printing press, about 4,000 pages a day could be printed. This helped make books more readily available to the general population. It also allowed for other material to be quickly printed, such as newspapers, pamphlets and posters about news events. The availability of reading material meant more and more people began to read. And it became easier to communicate ideas and knowledge to a larger audience.

The biggest library in the world is the Library of Congress in Washington, DC. It has nearly 167 million items, including over 39 million books as well as items like maps and photographs. It has about 838 miles (1,349 kilometers) of bookshelves!
ORIENTFOOTAGE/GETTY IMAGES

ON THE FRONT PAGE

By the 1600s weekly newspapers similar to those we see today began to pop up around Europe and Japan. These papers had anywhere from 2 to 24 pages, and they reported on current events. But since the government kept a close eye on newspapers, they couldn't include any news that might criticize political leaders. This began to change in the mid-1700s, when Sweden's elected officials passed a law forbidding the government from censoring, or blocking, information from being printed in newspapers. And the idea of freedom of the press—the right to report news without the threat of being silenced by the government—soon spread to other places around the world, allowing people to publish and read news that was thorough and true.

OUT FRONT

By the mid-1800s, newspapers had become popular and accessible to a huge audience that relied on them to get the biggest news of the day. You may have heard the term *front-page news*, which refers to stories important enough to appear on the front page of a newspaper with a large headline and a photo. Events like the sinking of the *Titanic* or the assassination of an American president were captured on the front page of many newspapers. And besides passing along details to the people of the time, they became an important historical record of these events.

Switching It Up

While newspapers continue to be made today, the prevalence of computers, the internet and email has changed the business. News articles can be written quickly and uploaded to an online edition of a newspaper rather than appearing in a physical printed copy. With that, more and more people are reading articles online. Some statistics indicate that more than half of readers choose to read newspapers online rather than in print. And this has caused a drop in the number of print newspapers being published. In fact, media experts say about 100 newspapers go out of business each year in North America. These same experts suggest it's likely that print newspapers will disappear for good within the next decade, and digital papers will become the only form available.

The ancient Romans are said to have published the first kind of daily newspaper. The *Acta Diurna* (meaning "daily events") described births and deaths, as well as local events and ceremonies. Rather than being printed on paper, this early newspaper was carved into metal or stone and then placed in areas where Romans might come across it, like the market.

The SOS distress signal is used worldwide, and it's probably the most well-known example of Morse code. It consists of three dots for the first *S*, three dashes for the *O* and then three more dots for the second *S*. But the letters in SOS don't stand for anything in particular. They were chosen because the signal itself is distinctive with its three short, three long and three short sounds. SOS has now become an expression we often use for any kind of call for help.

• • • ▬ ▬ ▬ • • •

Message Received

Long-distance communication made huge strides with the invention of the electric telegraph by American Samuel Morse in the 1830s. This device used electricity to send coded messages over a metal wire, which then had to be decoded, or translated, to be understood by the person at the other end of the wire. To send messages, Morse developed a special system that came to be called Morse code. It uses dots (short signals) and dashes (long signals) to represent numbers and letters of the alphabet. A message would be tapped out in Morse code on a ***transmitter***. This sent electrical ***currents*** through the wire to a part called a ***receiver***. That's where the person on the other end could get and decode the message.

By the end of the 1800s, networks of telegraph lines were found in countries throughout the world. In fact, a British engineer and his team successfully installed a telegraph cable along the bottom of the Atlantic Ocean from a coastal town in Ireland to a town called Heart's Content in Newfoundland in 1866. It was first used by governments and the military. But eventually European immigrants were able to send messages along it from North America to their families back home.

TETRA IMAGES/GETTY IMAGES

TRINITY BAY
GORGON
NIAGARA
AGAMEMNON
VALOROUS
VALENTIA BAY

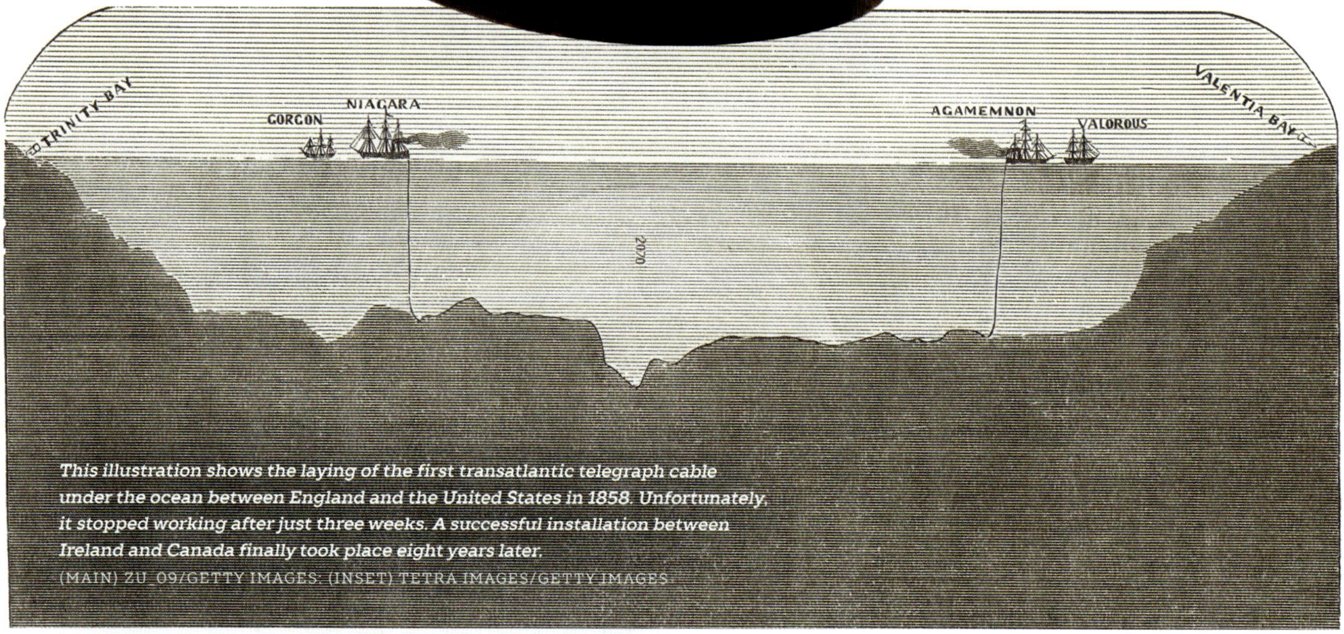

This illustration shows the laying of the first transatlantic telegraph cable under the ocean between England and the United States in 1858. Unfortunately, it stopped working after just three weeks. A successful installation between Ireland and Canada finally took place eight years later.

(MAIN) ZU_09/GETTY IMAGES; (INSET) TETRA IMAGES/GETTY IMAGES

Morse code is a sound-based language that conveys messages by using long and short signals that represent the alphabet and numbers. Funnily enough, some musicians have used Morse code as a sound effect in their songs.
OLGA CHUPRINA/GETTY IMAGES

Ahoy there! Alexander Graham Bell thought the best way to answer a phone call was to say "ahoy." But inventor Thomas Edison went with "hello" when answering calls in the early 1900s. And his greeting was the one that stuck.

According to recent statistics, about seven billion people around the world own a smartphone.
AMIR MUKHTAR/GETTY IMAGES

There's a Caller on the Line

Inventor Alexander Graham Bell took the technology of the telegraph and found a way to use it to send the sound of a voice from one place to another. With that he invented the first working telephone and gave people the ability to communicate with speech over long distances. A real game changer! His phone turned the sound of a voice into an electrical signal and then back into a sound once it reached the other end of the wire. As for the first phone call? That was made by Bell on March 10, 1876, when he phoned his assistant, Thomas Watson, who was in another room. It was short and sweet: "Mr. Watson, come here. I want to see you."

By 1877 the first telephone line had been constructed, and just three years later, nearly 50,000 telephones were being used across the United States. That number skyrocketed by 1910, when about six million telephones were being used for communication throughout the country. And the number of telephone users only continued to grow as phone lines eventually connected continents. In a matter of a few decades, the telephone became the fastest way for people across the globe to communicate with one another.

SEE YA, SMARTPHONES

Landline telephones remained popular for years. Things changed in the early 2000s. That's when cell phones and then smartphones arrived on the scene. Today many people have chosen to get rid of those home telephones that rely on landlines. Instead smartphones have become the chosen way to stay in touch. In fact, there are about seven billion smartphone users around the world today. But experts say that even the beloved smartphone may become a thing of the past eventually. And some suggest that smart glasses may replace them.

These special glasses will allow you to see digital information about objects as you're looking at them. For instance, if a friend comes into view, the glasses will gather up all the information they can find about them, from their name to their social media profiles. This info will be projected onto one of the glasses' lenses, allowing you to view it instantly. This kind of tech is known as augmented reality. Smart glasses are already out in the world, but they can't give you information about people you cross paths with…yet. Instead they take data from your smartphone, displaying information like texts, emails or maps on the lens for the wearer to see. But as technology advances, smart glasses will likely be able to do everything your smartphone can do. And that could mean you simply won't need or use your phone anymore.

Imagine what the future would look like if you could slip on a pair of glasses and see all types of information on the lenses or even use them to send emails or make phone calls!
SUE BARR/GETTY IMAGES

Phones have come a very long way from the one Alexander Graham Bell invented. Here's a look at the evolution of the telephone.

Box telephone: One of Bell's first phones, it had a transmitter and receiver. When he spoke into the mouthpiece of the device, his voice was converted into an electric current that traveled along a wire to a receiver where it was changed back to sound. This was the first type of telephone to go on sale.

DIVISION OF WORK AND INDUSTRY, NATIONAL MUSEUM OF AMERICAN HISTORY, SMITHSONIAN INSTITUTION

Switchboard: In 1878 the first switchboard opened in Connecticut. A switchboard was used to connect phone lines. When someone wanted to make a phone call, they had to first call the ***switchboard operator***. The operator then connected their call by removing and inserting electric plugs into a large control panel. This "switched" the phone call to the proper person.

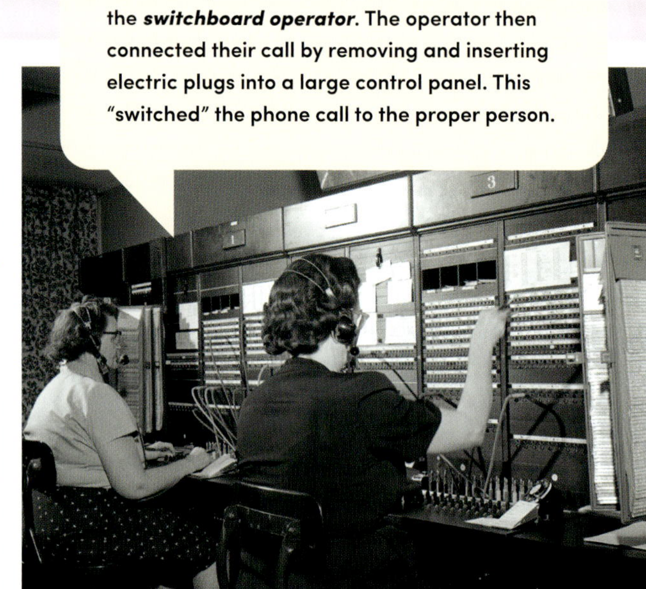

H. ARMSTRONG ROBERTS/GETTY IMAGES

DOUG4537/GETTY IMAGE

Candlestick: This phone was common from about 1890 to the 1940s. It was an upright telephone that featured a mouthpiece on top of its stand. The receiver was held up to the ear by the user during the conversation.

Rotary phone: The rotary dial system was invented in the late 1800s but became more commonly used by the 1920s. By the 1980s the push-button, or touch-tone, keypad was a more popular choice in homes. So if you hear someone say they're going to "dial" a number, that goes way back to the rotary phone.

WIN-INITIATIVE/NELEMAN/GETTY IMAGES

Cell phone: The telephone went wireless in 1973 when a team of engineers unveiled the cellular phone. This handheld phone used radio signals to make and receive calls. At the time, the phone weighed 2.5 pounds (1.13 kilograms), gaining it the nickname the Brick. Today there are cell phones so small, they're built into watches.

LOCKIECURRIE/GETTY IMAGES

MASKOT/GETTY IMAGES

Smartphone: This device took the idea of the cell phone and kicked it up a notch. The smartphone has a computer inside, which means it can do more than just make phone calls. It's also able to perform tasks like send and receive emails, play games and view audio and video files. The first smartphone was unveiled in 1993.

Two-way radios were first developed during World War II. The portable gadgets helped soldiers stay in constant contact. Once the war ended, the devices—commonly known as walkie-talkies—began to be used by the public and in businesses.
WESTEND61/GETTY IMAGES

Something in the Air

As the telephone found its way into people's homes, our focus on communication continued to develop. In 1895 an Italian scientist named Guglielmo Marconi invented a radio-like device that enabled a form of wireless communication. Originally used by sailors on ships at sea, Marconi's technology sent signals through the air using radio waves. Before this, sailors had relied on handheld flags to send information from a distance. A sailor would position flags at certain angles to represent letters and numbers. To receive the dispatch, a sailor in the distance had to use a telescope to "read" the flag message, then use their own flag to relay the communication to another sailor. With Marconi's new technology, sailors had a reliable form of quick communication. And communicating through radio waves was soon used on land as well.

Home Is Where the News Is

Marconi's invention eventually evolved from being used solely to send signals. Others, including Canadian inventor Reginald Fessenden, found ways to use Marconi's technology to transmit voices over radio waves. In 1920 a radio station in Pittsburgh, Pennsylvania, ***broadcast*** the first spoken news report. Soon there were hundreds of radio stations sending out news, music and entertainment shows across the airwaves. During the 1930s and 1940s—which is now known as the Golden Age of Radio—most households across the world had a radio on hand.

With newscasts becoming commonplace on the radio, the way people received information changed. Stories could be broadcast to huge audiences over the radio as they unfolded. One of the best examples of this takes us back to September 3, 1939. This marked the beginning of World War II. And on that day, then British prime minister Neville Chamberlain made a five-minute radio broadcast announcing that the country was at war. As the battles raged on, radio stations around the world sent teams of people to war zones to provide coverage. Some stations broadcast information 24 hours a day. And when the war officially ended in 1945, this news was announced to audiences on radio stations around the world. People didn't have to leave home to receive the biggest news of the day.

During the Golden Age of Radio, families gathered around the radio in their homes to listen to entertainment shows and get the latest news.
GEORGE MARKS/GETTY IMAGES

Watch What Happens

The ability to access the world's news was also made possible by the arrival of another method of broadcasting communication—the television. A young American inventor named Philo Farnsworth designed the electronic television in the late 1920s. About a decade later, his invention found its way into people's homes. The TV took over from radio as the main source of news in households. Instead of listening to news unfolding, people could watch it happening, getting the opportunity to see history in the making. For instance, a live broadcast of the Apollo 11 spacecraft *Eagle* landing on the moon in 1969 was watched by an astounding 600 million people around the world. And moments that were more horrific than awe-inspiring appeared on our screens as well. When New York City's World Trade Center was attacked on September 11, 2001, viewers both near and far watched the footage live. The television became a tool we could rely on to show us scenes from around the world, communicating information in real time.

Today television news gives us continual live feeds and first-person accounts of stories as they happen. We are all likely familiar with the term *breaking news*, which refers to live coverage of an event that is currently happening or has just happened. These unexpected reports may interrupt a show we're watching and evolve right there on our screens.

Don't Stop Now

Tracing the evolution of communication from the printing press to telephones to TV reminds us how focused humans have been—and still are—on finding new and improved ways to communicate. It might make you wonder why we keep searching for new ways to stay in touch when we have perfectly good methods already. Partly it seems to be about convenience and coming up with the quickest way to share as much information as possible. But it also might be that humans are curious and simply wired to invent things. Unlike any other creature on the planet, humans seem driven to come up with new ideas. And, as you'll see, we're not slowing down.

What new technologies will we come up with in the future? Only time will tell!
TARA MOORE/GETTY IMAGES

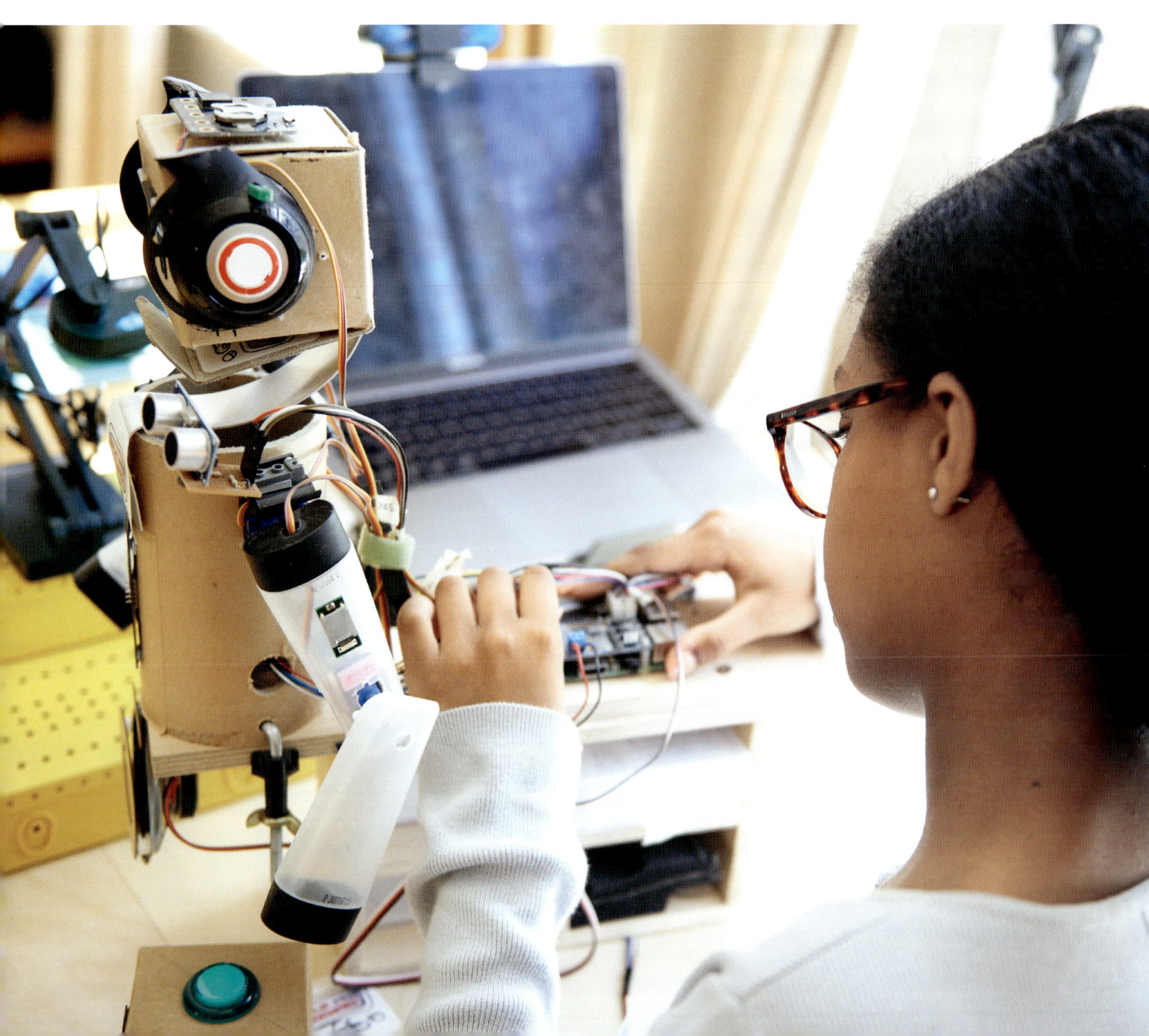

1945
First computer
(so big it filled
a room)
TODAY
12 million texts
sent every minute
FUTURE
Hologram
conversations
1989
Launch of the
internet as we
know it today
HOME
WORK
2020
Unequal access
to online learning
during the
COVID-19 pandemic

COMPUTERS RULE

Human communication changed forever when personal computers arrived in our homes. While the first computers were around in the mid-1800s, they weren't much like the computers we know today. By the 1940s, electronic computers had been developed—but they filled an entire room! Over time the machines got smaller and smaller, until we were able to have them in our homes. Personal computers started to become common during the 1980s. And once they got within our four walls, the way we communicated evolved and changed forever. Computers got more advanced with each passing decade, and before long smartphones had come along. Now it's hard to imagine how we ever survived without this technology.

What a Web We've Weaved

Personal computers, as well as smartphones and other devices, allow for a whole new way to receive news and information. And it's all thanks to the groundbreaking invention known as the internet—a network that connects computers around the world so that information can be shared between them. An early version of the internet was created in 1969, and it was used in the United States to allow the government and certain businesses to share information between computers. The internet as we use it came to be in 1989. That's when a computer scientist named Tim Berners-Lee invented the World Wide Web. It's a collection of websites that we can access, via the internet, on all our devices, including computers, tablets, smartphones and watches. By linking to these websites, we can get unlimited news and information. It's all at our fingertips and can be found in a matter of seconds.

It's the next best thing to being there! Some smartphone apps allow us to connect with one or more people in real time.
JAVIER ZAYAS PHOTOGRAPHY/GETTY IMAGES

A NEED FOR SPEED

It's a matter of seconds for many of us, but not for everyone. In some places, high-speed internet simply isn't available. Take rural parts of Canada, for instance. While more than 90 percent of the country's population can easily surf the internet, only about 60 percent of people in remote parts of the country have high-speed internet. And this number is even lower in Indigenous communities, where only some 40 percent of households have access to it.

So why does internet speed matter? The internet has become essential in modern-day life. It goes beyond providing us with news. We depend on it for everything from connecting with family and doctors to running businesses. For students, it's a place for research, a way to get in touch with educators and even take online courses. You may remember when the COVID-19 pandemic stopped the world in its tracks in 2020. Many kids had to switch to online learning, and for students without high-speed internet, it was impossible to connect and learn. Many governments are working toward making access to speedy internet service available to everyone, including people in remote places as well as to those who can't afford the service, so that we all have the ability to communicate and stay connected.

A selfie is a photo of yourself, alone or with other people. The world's first selfie is believed to have been snapped by an American photographer in 1839, when he used a camera to take a self-portrait in his family's store.
AJ_WATT/GETTY IMAGES

With news coming at us from more and more places, it's important to pay close attention to where we're getting our news and whether or not it's accurate. Sometimes things aren't always as they seem. Consider the following examples.

Does this mean war? Back in October 1938, getting the day's news over the radio was still a new concept. And that led to an epic moment of confusion for listeners across the United States. As a Halloween special, an American actor and director named Orson Welles broadcast an adaptation of a science fiction book called *The War of the Worlds*. The novel was the story of a Martian invasion of Earth. Welles decided to perform the book's retelling like a series of breaking news bulletins. The problem? Many listeners didn't catch the opening of the show, so they thought it was a real news story and that the country was under an alien attack. Not surprisingly, they began to panic, and some called the police. Welles became front-page news himself the next morning for his radio fiasco, and he had to publicly apologize for causing such a frenzy.

ACME NEWS PHOTOS/WIKIMEDIA COMMONS/PUBLIC DOMAIN

A deep fake-out: While Welles's actions weren't intentional, today we're beginning to see deliberate attempts to spread false news and information. Take the emergence of ***deepfakes*** in 2017. These are images and video recordings that have been altered on a computer to replace real footage and audio of a person's face and/or voice with someone else's. This makes it appear as if the person is saying or doing things that they never did. Deepfakes can look authentic enough to fool just about anyone.

Often deepfakes are made for entertainment purposes. For example, they may place celebrities in movie scenes they were never part of. That's all fun and games. But deepfakes are also used to spread false information, and there are growing concerns about how this technology could be used. In 2018 someone created a realistic deepfake of former US president Barack Obama commenting on the dangers of fake news. It wasn't really him, but people believed it was a real video. This example shows us how dangerously convincing a deepfake can be and how easily we can be misled.

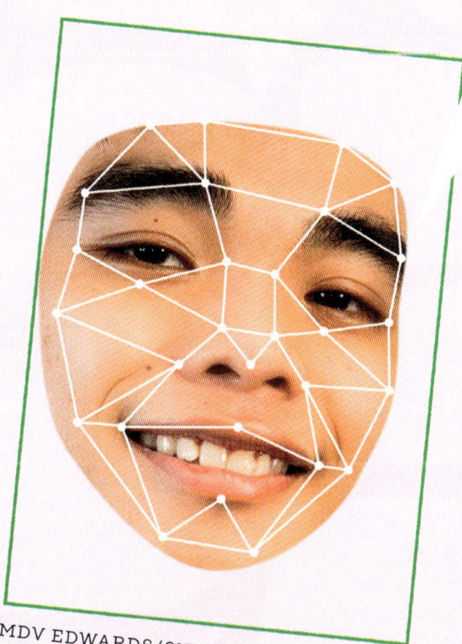

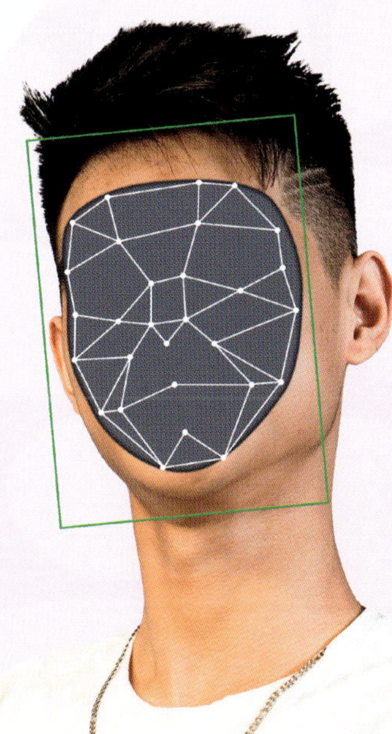

MDV EDWARDS/SHUTTERSTOCK.COM

A server room is a place where computer hardware is stored, powered and operated. Many computer systems are connected to the equipment in this room. It's usually a place that is secure and air-conditioned to keep devices from overheating.

H. ARMSTRONG ROBERTS/GETTY IMAGES

It's All about the Inbox

The internet helps people do some serious communicating. By using email, we can send and receive messages to people all over the world in an instant. The first ever email was sent in 1971. Today, as you read in an earlier chapter, *billions* of emails are sent each day. That's a whole lot of communication! But while this electronic mail can reach its destination in a matter of seconds, that doesn't mean it's a perfect method of communication. Research has found that the majority of people have plenty of unread emails in their inbox. Often those emails aren't being ignored but are left to be read at a later time. That time sometimes never comes, as more and more new emails drop into the inbox each day and those older ones get forgotten.

You can choose to send a text to just one person or a whole bunch of people. In a group text, all the recipients of the message can view and respond to the texts that are sent.
MASKOT/GETTY IMAGES

Neurologists—experts who study the brain and nervous system—have found that texting can be helpful in identifying when someone is having a medical issue. There have been several instances of people sending a jumbled text message while they were having a stroke—that's a sudden illness in which the blood supply to the brain is interrupted, sometimes just for a few seconds. Like slurred speech, researchers say, garbled text messaging—known as dystextia—can now be considered a symptom of a stroke.

IDK How That Happened So Quickly

There's another form of communication that allows us to connect instantly—text messaging. Texting lets us send electronic messages to each other over mobile devices. The first text message was sent by a young engineer named Neil Papworth, from his computer, in December 1992. His simple message, *Merry Christmas*, was delivered to a co-worker's cell phone. At that time, his colleague couldn't respond to the text because cell phones didn't have the capability to send messages. That changed a year later, when the first cell phone with the ability to text was invented.

Fast-forward to life today, and experts say at least 12 million texts are sent every *minute* of the day on smartphones! And that number doesn't even include the texts sent on apps designed specifically for online chatting, so the number is actually much higher. Just like that, it seems, texting has become one of the most widely used forms of communication to date, alongside email and social media. The ability to text has sparked an interesting change in how we choose to communicate. Most of us tend to spend more time texting than talking on the phone. And we generally reply to a text within a few minutes. All this has led to our phones, which were originally designed for speaking to each other, taking on a different purpose and the emergence of a different way of "talking." And, as we learned earlier, it's sparked the evolution of a new language—textese—that sees us using abbreviations like BTW (by the way), IDK (I don't know) and and IMO (in my opinion) in our texting conversations.

Getting under Your Skin

With all that being said, it might seem like we've gone as far as we can go when it comes to communication and our devices. After all, what other ideas could we possibly come up with? But if we've learned anything, it's that humans are unstoppable. We're always eager to come up with new and innovative ideas. So what does the future of communication look like? Here's one possibility: communication implants. Some forward thinkers suggest we might be able to implant circuits in the hand, so that its palm would become a keyboard for a device like a smartphone or tablet. It sounds unbelievable, but there are already thousands of people who have rice-sized microchips inserted under the skin in their hands to use as a key. They can swipe their hand over a digital reader outside their home or office and, voilà, the door unlocks. So perhaps having gadgetry under our skin to help us communicate more quickly is a real possibility down the road.

We Still Have a Lot to Say

One thing is clear: we sure know how to communicate! If you look at the world around you, you'll see other forms of communication that haven't been mentioned in this book. Consider street signs and traffic lights. Both are nonverbal forms of communication that help us get around easily. And then there's the world of social media. Statistics tell us that about five billion people (and growing!) use social media platforms like Snapchat, YouTube and Instagram to share ideas, get news and connect with one another. Add to this the methods we've already discussed, like texting and email, and it's clear we have access to constant communication at our fingertips.

Born for This

And we're not finished when it comes to finding new ways to communicate. Technology is continually changing, and with these advances comes new ideas. Whether it's "talking" with our brains or meeting up with a hologram version of our friend, who knows what other ways we may find to connect with each other? It's remarkable that humans have gone from gestures to talking and writing, and from the telephone to the computer, and never looked back…only forward.

Why is this? Many experts say we are born to come together and connect. Matthew Lieberman, a renowned psychologist who studies human behavior, is one of them. He says this need to connect and build relationships is as vital to humans as our need for food and shelter. So perhaps that explains why humans have discovered such a variety of ways to communicate with each other throughout history and why we continue to search for new methods of communication.

One of the newest ways for people to communicate is by creating podcasts. A podcast is an audio recording that can be made about any topic.
SEVENTYFOUR/GETTY IMAGES

Sometimes we get so caught up with our devices, we forget to connect with those who are in the same room. Can you relate?
JGI/JAMIE GRILL/GETTY IMAGES

Let's Talk It Out

But here's the big question. Are we actually better communicators thanks to all the ways we've found to stay in touch? It's complicated. While we may be connected, we seem to be stepping away from face-to-face exchanges. Instead we often rely on typed words and even emojis or GIFs to get our points across rather than our voices. This can lead to brief interactions and fewer meaningful conversations. We can communicate more easily, thanks to technology, but we're not always making a genuine connection with the person on the other end of our device.

PHUB AND SNUB

Some studies, including those done by Genavee Brown, a psychology professor at Northumbria University in England, suggest that although our devices help us stay more connected to people who are physically far away from us, they seem to separate us from those who are physically nearby. That's because our devices tend to attract our attention and get in the way of our face-to-face conversations. This ends up limiting how much we interact with those who are right in front of us. There's even a term for this: phubbing. That's snubbing or ignoring someone who's nearby while you focus on your phone. Maybe you've noticed this behavior yourself. Sometimes it's hard to set aside devices and ignore them completely.

Keep It Going

Will our approach change anytime soon? Probably not. Most of us are unlikely to give up our devices and the ease of communicating that comes with them. So what's the lesson here? There's no denying that our devices are extremely useful for communication, but perhaps it's worth thinking about how we choose to communicate. After all, if the past has shown us anything, it's that no matter how we evolve and change, humans want to connect with each other. And sometimes that can be done in the simplest way, with the people who are right beside us.

There's a time and place for everything. Spending time together without our devices is always a good idea!
PIXELSEFFECT/GETTY IMAGES

THOMAS BARWICK/GETTY IMAGES

GLOSSARY

adolescence—the period of life between childhood and adulthood

amplify—to make louder

anatomy—the internal and external structures of the body and how they work together

ancestor—a member of your family who lived long ago

archaeologists—scientists who study ancient humans by looking at objects from their past lives and activities

audio—of or relating to sound

broadcast—to send out or transmit, such as a program on TV or radio

civilizations—groups of people who live together in one area and develop their own culture and way of life

communication—the sharing and exchanging of information, ideas or messages

couriers—people who deliver packages and messages

currents—flows of electrical energy moving from one place to another

deepfakes—videos that have been manipulated using computer technology to show real people doing and saying things they never did or said

emojis—digital symbols used in electronic messages that represent objects, ideas and emotions

evaporated—changed from a liquid into a vapor

genes—the parts of the body's cells that determine traits such as eye color, height and hair color

gestures—movements of the body that communicate ideas or attitudes

heliographic messaging—transmitting messages by reflecting sunlight from a mirror

hieroglyphics—a writing system used by ancient Egptians that used pictures and symbols rather than letters or words

Homo sapiens—the scientific name for humankind

internet—a network that connects computers around the world so that information can be shared between them, allowing people to communicate and keep in touch

language—the system that people use to communicate or share information. This can include speaking, writing and gesturing.

larynx—the voice box, the organ in your neck that helps produce vocal sounds

linguists—people who study language

migrate—to move from one country or region to another

navigate—to find your way from place to place

prehistoric—existing in a time before there were written records

receiver—a device that receives electrical signals and then turns them back into the original sounds

scribe—a writer and record keeper in ancient times

slang—an informal language consisting of words and phrases that are not part of the standard vocabulary

steganography—the technique of hiding messages inside or on top of something that is not secret

switchboard operator—a person who connects phone calls

text messaging—sending short messages electronically, usually between cell phones

transmitter—a device that turns talking or other information into electric signals

vocabulary—a collection of words used to communicate with others

RESOURCES

Print

Challen, Paul, Shipa Mehta-Jones, Lynn Peppas and Hazel Richardson. *Communication in the Ancient World.* Crabtree Publishing Company, 2011.

Chrisp, Peter, Joe Fullman, Susan Kennedy and Philip Parker. *History Year by Year: The History of the World, from Stone Age to the Digital Age.* DK Publishing, 2013.

Harari, Yuval Noah. *Unstoppable Us, Volume 1: How Humans Took Over the World.* Puffin Canada, 2022.

Richards, Mary. *A History of Words for Children.* Thames & Hudson, 2022.

Webb, Mick. *The Book of Languages: Talk Your Way around the World.* Owlkids Books, 2015.

Woolf, Alex. *Smoke Signals to Smartphones: A Timeline of Long-Distance Communication.* World Book, 2016.

Online

BBC: History for Kids: bbc.co.uk/history/forkids/index.shtml

Britannica Kids: kids.britannica.com

CBC Kids: cbc.ca/kids

DK Find Out! dkfindout.com/us

Exploratorium: exploratorium.edu/explore

History Classroom: history.com/classroom

History for Kids: historyforkids.net

Kids Discover: online.kidsdiscover.com

Kids Work! History of Telecommunications: knowitall.org/document/history-telecommunications-kids-work

National Geographic Education: education.nationalgeographic.org

Odyssey Online: carlos.emory.edu/htdocs/ODYSSEY/index.html

Ology: American Museum of Natural History: amnh.org/explore/ology

Smithsonian for Kids: si.edu/kids

The Conversation: Curious Kids: theconversation.com/ca/topics/curious-kids-36782

Time for Kids: timeforkids.com

Wonderopolis: wonderopolis.org

ACKNOWLEDGMENTS

Many thanks to the entire pod at Orca Book Publishers, especially my editor, Kirstie Hudson, for her help in shaping this book, as well as Dahlia Yuen for the creative design work. And huge thanks to illustrator Xulin for their wonderful art. And, as always, thank you to Sam and Grace, who I'd listen to any minute of the day.

INDEX

*Page numbers in **bold** indicate an image caption.*

advertising industry, 31
alphabets, 46
amplify, voice, 36, 81
anatomy, 7, 10, 81
ancestors, earliest
  ability to speak, 3, 5, 7–8
  defined, 81
  gestures of, 5
  language, 17–19
ancient cultures
  alphabets, 46
  couriers, 34, 48
  mail services, **40**, 50–51
  secret messages, 49
  spoken languages, 23
  use of beacons, 30–32, 34
  use of sounds, 35–36
  written languages, 42–44
animal communication, 22, 27, 34, **41**, 47
Apollo 11 moon landing, **54**, 66
archaeologists, 12, 31, 81
archaic words, 24
artificial intelligence (AI), **28**, 39
audio, 13, 81
  See also sounds

babies
  and gestures, 14
  language development, 23
  and mother's voice, **4**, 13
beacons, 30–34
Bell, Alexander Graham, 60, 62
Berners-Lee, Tim, 70
body language
  facial expressions, 6, 45
  gestures, 5, 6, 14, 27, 81
  tone of voice, 6, 23
braille, **40**, 46
Braille, Louis, **40**, 46
brain-to-brain interface, **5**, 15
broadcast media, 65–66, 81
Byzantine Empire, 32

Cabo Vilán lighthouse, **32**
Canada
  access to internet, 72
  and Indigenous cultures, 20
car computers, 47
cars (traffic), 38, 77
cell phones, **55**, 61, 63, 75
censorship of the press, 57
chemical signal messages, 27
China, ancient, 30, 49
civilizations, 1, 46, 81
coded messages. *See* secret messages
coding languages, 47
communication
  defined, 81
  forms of, 1–2, 55, 69
  information overload, 70, 73, 74
  social interaction, 1, **9**, 75, 77–79
computers
  artificial intelligence (AI), 39
  brain-to-brain interface, **5**, 15
  in cars, 47
  coding languages, 47
  digital bioacoustics, 46
  history of, **68**, 69–76
  voice-recognition systems, 10
  See also internet
conversations
  electronic devices, 1, 58–67, 71
  face-to-face, 3, 45, 78
  and gestures, **14**
  language translation, 26
  meaningful, 78–79
  need for, 1, **3**, **9**
  use of filler words, 25
  use of text words, 17, 25
couriers
  defined, 81
  homing pigeons, 34
  types of, 48–53
COVID-19 pandemic, **68**, 72
cultural genocide, 20–21
cuneiform, **40**, 42

deepfakes, 73, 81
drumming, 35

earbuds, 26
education
  access to internet, 72
  of the deaf, 22
Egypt, ancient
  hieroglyphics, 42, 44, 46, 81
  Lighthouse of Alexandria, **32**
  and voice research, **4**, 12
email, 52, 57, 74
emojis, 44–45, 81
England, 19, 36, 52
English language, **16**, 19, 26
Esperanto, 18

face-to-face interactions, 1, 3, 45, 78
facial expressions, 6, 45
fake news, 73
Farnsworth, Philo, 66
France, 50
fruit bats, 47

Galápagos Islands, 53
gestures, 5, 6, 14, 27, 81
global positioning systems (GPS), **28**, 32
Greeks, ancient
  alphabet, 46
  sending messages, 34, 49
  use of megaphones, 36

Gutenberg, Johannes, **54**, 56

heliographic messaging, 34, 81
hieroglyphics, 42, 44, 46, 81
Hill, Rowland, 52
holograms, 3, **68**, 77
homing pigeons, 34
Homo sapiens, 18, 81
honeybees, 27
horns, 36–38
humans, prehistoric
  ability to speak, 3, 5, 7–8
  defined, 82
  gestures of, 5
  language, 17–19

implants, **15**, 76
Inca Empire, 48
Indigenous
  languages, **6**, 20–21
  signals, 31, 34, 36
Indigenous communities, internet access, 72
information overload
  emails, 74
  false news, 73
internet
  dangers of technology, 73
  defined, 81
  email, 52, 57, 74
  history of, 2, **68**, 70–74
  impact on print news, 57
  online learning, **68**, 72
  podcasts, **77**
  social media, 61, 72, 77
  unequal access, 72
  See also computers

Khan, Genghis, 34
Klingon language, **16**, 22

language
  defined, 81
  families of, 19
  loss of, 20–21
  visual forms, 6, 44–45
  See also spoken languages; written language systems
language barriers
  and translation, 26
  use of shorthand and symbols, 23, 25
larynx, 11, **12**, 81
Latin alphabet, 46
Library of Congress, **56**
Lighthouse of Alexandria, **32**
lighthouses, **28**, 32
Lingit people, 20
linguists, 17, 18, 22, 81
literacy, 36, 42, 56–57
long-distance communication
  couriers, 48–51
  earliest forms, 2, 30–36
  marine, 32, 64
  Morse code, **54**, 58, **59**
Lord of the Rings, The, 22

mail
  electronic, 52, 57, 74
  postal services, **40**, 50–53
Mandarin, 20
Marconi, Guglielmo, 64–65
marine
  flag signals, 64
  navigation, 32
mass media
  early forms of, 36, 57
  newspapers, 56–57
  radio and television, 65–66, 73
  real time news, 66–67, 70, 73
  social media, 61, 72, 77
  and world events, **54**, 57, 65, 66
megaphones, 36, 37
migrate, 18–19, 81
military, use of signals, 30–31, 58, **64**
Minoans, ancient, 34
mobile devices
  AI assistants, 39
  real time news, 66–67, 70, 73
  wearable, **39**, **54**, 61
  See also smartphones
Morse code, **54**, 58, **59**
musical instruments, 35–37

navigate, 32, 82
news. *See* mass media
newspapers, 56–57
Nicaragua, 22
nonverbal communication
  defined, 29
  facial expressions, 6, 45
  gestures, 5, 6, 14, 27, 81
  street signs, 77
  See also long-distance communication

Obama, Barack deepfake videos, 73
Odawa Nation, 36

peacocks, 27
pencils, **43**
Persian Empire, **40**, 50
photography, **72**, 73
pictograms, 44–45
pigeons, homing, 34
podcasts, **77**
Ponca people, 34
Port Lockroy, Antarctica, **40**, 53
postal services, **40**, 50–53
postcards, **52**
prairie dogs, 27
prehistoric humans
  ability to speak, 3, 5, 7–8
  defined, 82
  gestures of, 5
  language, 17–19
printing press, **54**, 56–57

radio broadcast, fiasco, 73
radio signals, 64–65
resources, 83
Romans, ancient, 49, 51, 57

rural internet access, 72

Scotland, beacon, **33**
scribes, 42, 82
secret messages
  heliographic, 34
  steganography, 49, 82
signal fires, 32, **33**
signals
  use of sound, 35–39
  visual, 29–34
sign languages, 6, **7**, 22
skywriting, **28**, 31
slang, 24, 82
smart glasses, **54**, 61
smartphones
  and text messaging, **68**, 75, 78–79
  use of, 25, **60**, 63
smartwatches, **39**
smoke signals, 30–32
social interaction, 1, **9**, 75, 77–79
social media, 61, 72, 77
sounds
  amplified voice, 36
  instruments, 35–37
  in language, 7–8, 10–11, 23
  tone of voice, 6, 23
Spain, lighthouse, **32**
speech
  evolution of, **4**, 5, 7–8
  unique voice print, **10**
  vocal tract, 7, 10–12, 13, **48**
  voice, **4**, 13
spoken languages
  banning of, 20–21
  changes to, 24, 25
  endangered, 20–21
  Esperanto, 18
  history of, 17–19
  linguists, 17, 18, 22, 81
  made-up, 22
  translation, 26
  unusual, 23
  use of filler words, 25
Star Trek, 22
Star Wars, 22
steganography, 49, 82
Sumerians, ancient, 42
switchboard operator, 62, 82
symbols
  braille, **40**, 46
  pictograms, 44–45

tablets, ancient and modern, 42, 51
technology
  dangers of, 73
  early inventions, 2, 32, 34, 36
  electronic devices, 58–67
  global positioning systems (GPS), 32
  holograms, 3, **68**, 77
  implants, **15**, 76
  and innovation, 3, 55, 67
  and language translation, 26
  printing press, **54**, 56–57
  voice-recognition, 10
  wearable, **39**, **54**, 61
  See also computers; internet
telegraph, 58, 64
telephones
  AI assistants, 39
  cell phones, **55**, 61, 63, 75
  history of, 60–63, 73
  smartphones, 25, **60**, 63
television, 66
text messaging
  defined, 82
  impact of, **68**, 75, 78–79
  and language, **17**, 23, 25
town crier, 36
translation, advances, 26
trees, communication, 27

United States
  and Indigenous cultures, 20–21
  Library of Congress, **56**

Vatican smoke signal, **29**, 30
verbal communication. *See* speech; spoken languages
video footage manipulation, 73
Vikings, 19
vocabulary, 24, 82
vocalizations, animal, 27, 47
vocal tract, 7, 10–12, 13, **48**
voice
  amplified, 36, 81
  and helium, 13
  recognition by babies, **4**, 13
voice-activated devices, 39
voice recognition systems, 10

warfare
  impact on languages, 19
  and signals, 30–31, 58, **64**
War of the Worlds, The radio broadcast, 73
Welles, Orson, 73
West Africa, drumming, 35
whistling, 23
Wilcox, Marie, **16**, 21
words, new, 24
World Wide Web, 70
written communication
  postal services, **40**, 50–53
  and the printing press, 56–57
written language systems
  alphabets, 46
  computer code, 47
  emojis, 44–45
  hieroglyphics, 42, 44
  history of, 41–44, 46
  pencils, **43**
  text messaging, 17, 23, 82
Wukchumni language, 21

Yahgan people, 31
yodeling, **16**, 23
Yokut people, 21
Yoruba, 35

From the **PAST**

to the **PRESENT**

and into the **FUTURE!**

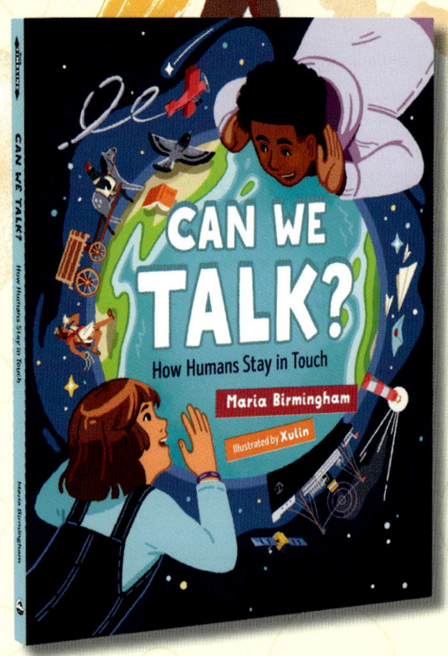

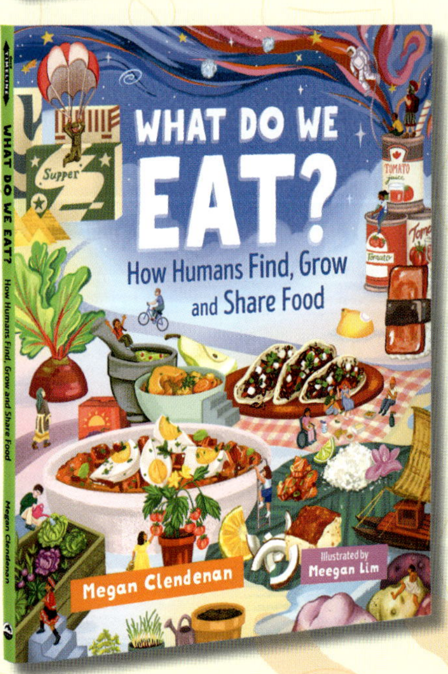

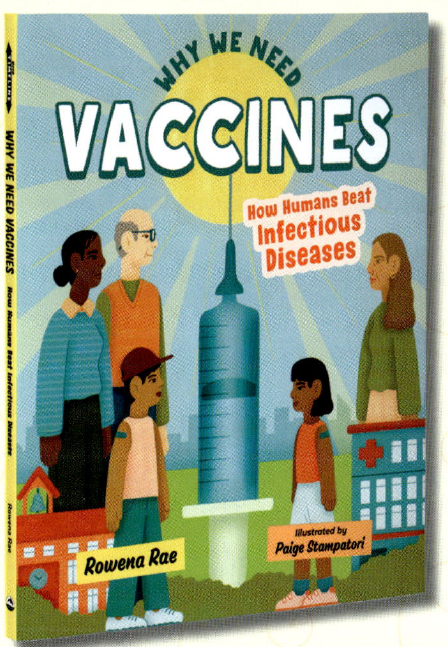

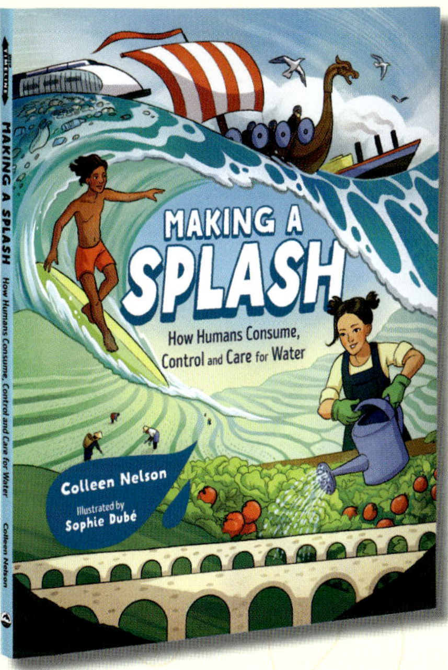

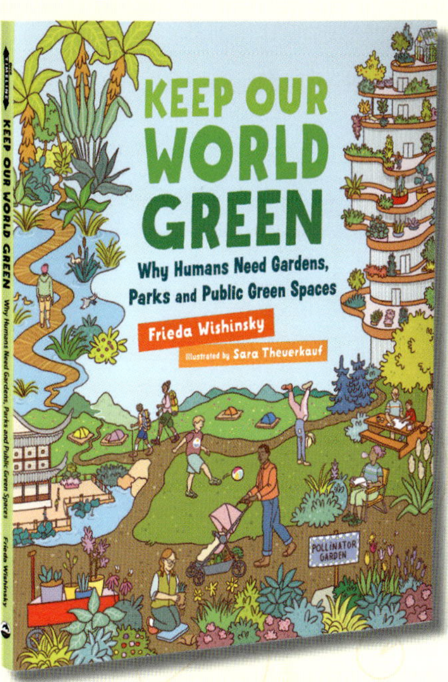

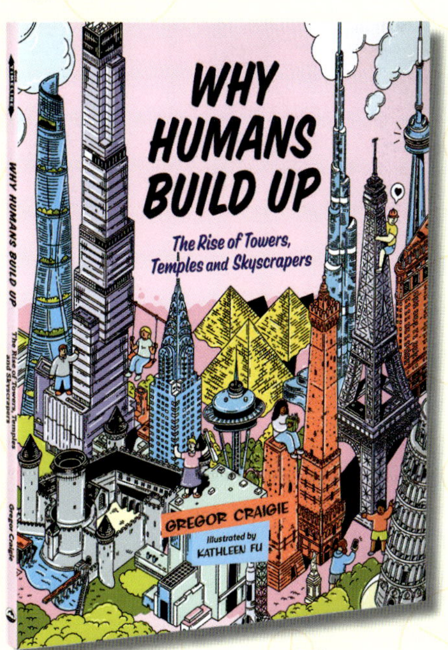

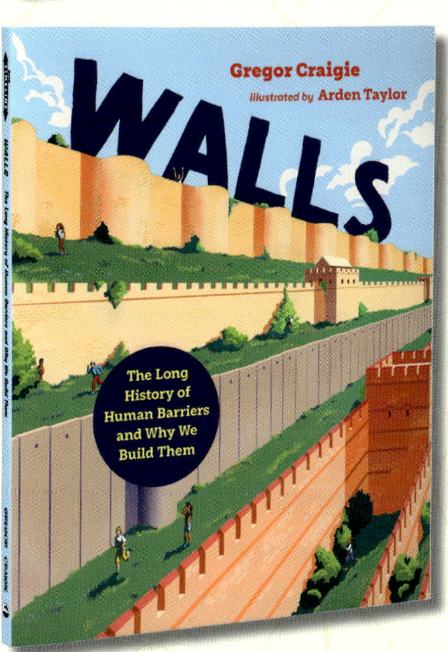

Codes

Time

School

Engineering

The Orca Timeline series explores how big ideas have shaped humanity. Discover what our collective history can tell us about the planet today and tomorrow.

Grace McDonald

Maria Birmingham has worked in the children's publishing industry for over 25 years. She is the award-winning author of several books for young people, including *Are We There Yet? How Humans Find Their Way* and *Are We Having Fun Yet? The Human Quest for a Good Time* in the Orca Timeline series. She lives with her family in Brampton, Ontario.

Andrew Love

Xulin is an award-winning Canadian Chinese illustrator, cartoonist, writer and muralist based in Toronto. They write and illustrate comics at the intersection of science and social justice. As a lifelong learner passionate about education and science communication, they've dedicated their career to translating complex ideas into compelling and understandable illustrations.